# Inside Guide to Training as a Teacher

**Also available from Continuum**

*How to Survive your First Year in Teaching* – Sue Cowley

*Guerilla Guide to Teaching* – Sue Cowley

*Trainee Teacher's Survival Guide* – Hazel Bennett

*100 Ideas for Trainee Teachers* – Angella Cooze

# Inside Guide to Training as a Teacher

*A Practical Survival Guide*

Jon Barbuti

continuum
LONDON • NEW YORK

**Continuum International Publishing Group**

The Tower Building
11 York Road
London
SE1 7NX

Suite 704
80 Maiden Lane
New York
NY 10038

**British Library Cataloguing-in-Publication Data**
A catalogue record for this book is available from the British Library.

ISBN: 0–8264–9031–X (paperback)

**Library of Congress Cataloging-in-Publication Data**
A catalog record for this book is available from the Library of Congress.

Typeset by Servis Filmsetting Ltd, Manchester
Printed and bound in Great Britain by
Antony Rowe Ltd, Chippenham, Wilts

# Contents

# Acknowledgements

The chance to write a book, especially one based on my own seemingly random observations, was a wonderful opportunity.

However, without the support of a number of people it would never have happened and so, without wishing to go all Gwyneth Paltrow, here is my list of thank yous.

Firstly, there are a few people on the course who helped me through the year. My tutor Malcolm provided a wealth of valuable information and also showed that there is no need for good teachers to be particularly organized. I also welcomed the chance to talk through problems with course mates, especially Steve and Steve (in no particular order). However, Steve could have stood his round slightly more often.

My family provided amazing support throughout the year. My brother Matt and his wife, Linda, both teachers, were a great source of knowledge, as was my sister Alex, though not necessarily on teaching. My mum and dad were great in backing my latest career venture – they'd back me if I said I was setting up a business selling sand in Blackpool.

But by far the most important person to thank is my gorgeous wife, Ali. Not only did she allow me to leave a perfectly good job and retrain even while we were planning a wedding, she also put up with all my late-night writing / Internet poker sessions.

# 1 The big change

Eight months ago, having knocked out one sports story too many, I decided it was time for a change. It was time to quit the world of online journalism, time to stock up on woolly sweaters from M & S and time to retrain as a primary school teacher.

Fortunately work didn't notice this – or if they did they were very good at not letting on – and continued to pay me while I went through the tortuous process of applying for a place on a course; filling in personal statements, hunting down exam certificates and ringing long-lost relatives to say 'I know I haven't spoken to you in ten years, but can you just check I didn't leave my birth certificate there . . .'

Eventually, though, all was sorted (note to self – don't use the word sorted when Ofsted are in . . . ) and so I arrived at Manchester Metropolitan University's Crewe Campus as one of 94 new recruits, all starting out on a journey that will lead from the safety of the lecture hall into the turmoil of a classroom crammed full with hyperactive youngsters.

And there is so much to be learnt – and not just the teaching techniques necessary to keep a classroom engaged in learning. As a former online journalist with a good A-level in maths, I'd naively thought that English, maths and ICT, all at the core of the curriculum, would take care of themselves. Needless to say, I was mistaken. Possibly, selective memory is a slight problem, but my recall suggested that a primary school English lesson consisted of a class full of kids writing a story about pretty much whatever they wanted. It didn't consist of a teacher explaining the structure of a cinquain (a poem consisting of 22 syllables) or encouraging the class to write a mnemonic aide memoir. Similarly, maths has moved on and, by age 11, children should be able to recognize that $70 + 71 + 75 + 77$ is the same as $70 \times 4 + 1 + 5 + 7$ and be able to solve it in their head! In short, the youngsters are getting smarter and they'll soon be nicking our jobs and putting us out to pasture.

However, before that happens there are a few years teaching to be fitted in and before that can happen there is a course to be completed. There are books to be read, 87 at the last count, lessons to be planned, tests to be taken and essays to be written, but the real learning will happen in class. Over the course of the next nine months I will spend almost 20 weeks in school, a huge amount of time, but will it be enough? At the moment, the thought of teaching for six hours a day, every day, is panic-inducing and 20 weeks does not seem all that long to turn anyone from complete beginner to competent teacher. That said, thousands of students go through the process every year and if people on *Faking It* can go from hairdressers to sheep shearers in a week (or was it the other way round), I'm sure I can crack teaching.

In any case, there is not enough time to worry. Next week I'll spend my first day in the school that, later on in the year, will become my home for two months and I can't wait. I think.

# 2  First steps

'So how did it go?' asked my partner as I slumped through the door, straightened out a neck cricked from bending over for six hours, started to scrape paint marks off my best (for best read only) tie and headed in the general direction of our alcohol collection. 'Fine,' I replied, at the same time putting my hand in my pocket and pulling out a soggy tissue given to me, quite possibly as a present, by a coldy, six-year-old girl. But, of course, fine, or fineurrghh as it came out, was a most unsatisfactory answer – tiring, nerve-racking, exciting, overwhelming, even plain old confusing would have been far better adjectives to describe my first day in class.

Arriving like a typical teacher, in a suit and car worth roughly equivalent amounts of money and sporting recently squashed glasses held together by superglue, I was taken on a tour of a school of such overwhelming size that I'd started to forget the beginning even before we were half way around. However, I had at least learnt the whereabouts of the essentials: the Year 1 classroom that will act as my base, the resources cupboard, the IT suite, the library, the gents toilets and, should it ever get a bit too much, the exit.

Perhaps the most useful of all the rooms in the morning was the gents for a quick spot of sponging down. Having finally opted for the smartness of a suit over the practicality of a jumper, I went straight into the first lesson of the day – and promptly found myself helping a group of wannabe Jackson Pollocks paint a Gruffalo (a terrible creature with knobbly knees, a spiky back, giant tusks and a wart on its nose).

The artwork, which tied into their literacy work on storytelling, helped show the importance of creating an enjoyable, lively atmosphere for the children to learn in. The Government has made testing the key to all teaching, but I have already realized that the good teachers have the confidence to go off on tangents to enhance their pupils' learning. Talking about a Gruffalo led the class to think of buffaloes, then of buffalo mozzarella and ended with a few given the task of helping a teacher to make buffalo mozzarella pizzas, developing planning, organization and turn-taking skills that will prove invaluable. It tasted pretty good as well.

A primary school day never follows a linear path. Most of the time, there are a variety of activities going on and even when the teacher is seemingly teaching a lesson to the whole class they are actually having to deliver three concurrent lessons – one for each of the three broad ability groups, ranging from the below average to those who need far more of a challenge. Already, I realize how hard the planning is going to be. Every child deserves an education that is relevant to their own ability, but planning 30 unique lessons for every hour of the day is clearly impractical.

At university I have already had my first taste of planning and delivering a lesson – honing my skills by trying to teach classmates about Japanese poetry. The lesson went well, everyone met the learning objectives, produced some poetry and not one of them put their hand up to say that the boy next to them had just done a 'blow off'.

I'm not expecting it to go quite as smoothly when I get to teach my first real lessons in a few weeks though, in fact if I can say it went 'fine', or even 'fineurrghh', I'll be pretty chuffed with myself.

# 3 Pre-course and interview

You've probably already got a place on a course, spent countless hours in school and feel ready and raring to get cracking with teacher training. And if that is the case, congratulations. You are going to love the course, meet some amazing people both in class and among your peers, learn more than in any other year of your life and experience a whole range of amazing highs and depressing lows. At the end of it you'll get a piece of paper that says you're a teacher. It's only a standard piece of A4 but with it is the chance to affect hundreds, if not thousands of lives. It's a bit like a winning lottery ticket, it looks innocuous but it symbolizes a complete lifestyle change.

Those of you with a place are the lucky ones. Just getting on the course was an achievement in itself, with dozens of people competing for every place. Indeed, according to one helpful girl I met pre-course, it's more like hundreds per place, though that might be a slight exaggeration. Only you're not lucky. You'll have been selected for the course because of your personality and your suitability, because of your experience and your potential, and because you stood out from the crowd. The only thing that definitely did not have anything to do with it was luck. The key to having got on the course was showing that, given time and the right training, you'll make an excellent teacher and that, unsurprisingly, is the key to anyone thinking of applying for the course. Paradoxically, it's fairly straightforward and bloody difficult.

Absolutely essential to anyone hoping to get on a course is to have spent some time in school. The time spent in school serves a dual purpose: it shows some commitment and should also help answer any doubts you have as to teaching as a profession.

There's no set amount of time you need to dedicate to observing lessons in a local school; it seems to me that it depends on your other commitments. Among my peers on the course, some had spent over a year as a teaching assistant (TA) and others had spent many months of their own time simply observing lessons in a variety of schools. While impressive and advantageous (and not to mention worrying when you're sat next to these people in interview), this level of experience is not entirely necessary. Prior to my interview, I had spent just two weeks observing lessons in a local school and had a further two weeks arranged elsewhere. Was I lazy or uncommitted – absolutely not, I just had to fit the time in as best I could by taking holidays from my job, making sure all the time that they thought I was actually taking a holiday and not scouting out future career moves. Using four of your five weeks annual holiday and spending a fortune on fake tan to complete the illusion of holidays in Barbados (I probably should have just said I was going to Prestatyn . . . ) shows just as much dedication to finding out about teaching as does earning a decent living as a TA or filling in a fairly uncluttered calendar with months in school.

This time in school, however short, is your chance to check that you really want to be a teacher. The workload on the course is demanding and I am reliably informed that it only gets harder once the transition is made from trainee to teacher. If you merely fancy doing the course as a way of filling a year or as an easy option, then now might be the time to reconsider. You get £6,000 to train, but divide that by the number of hours you'll have to work and the stress you'll encounter and it will soon become obvious that, as an easy option, it pales into insignificance compared to frying burgers or stacking shelves. And, incidentally, I know about such things, having spent many happy summers stacking shelves in a local supermarket and a whole week frying burgers for the drunkards of Maidstone (of which there are many).

During my pre-course time in school I tried to get around as many classes as possible. Although I was already certain that I would want to teach in Key Stage 2 (KS2) – probably because my own memories of time in the infants consist entirely of vomit (not my own), urine (not always my own) and fights in the sand pit – I made a point of visiting the infant classes, partly to check that I really did feel more suited to teaching juniors and partly so that I could talk intelligently about KS1 in interviews.

I found initially that it is easy to feel like a spare part in the classroom while observing lessons. The teacher carries on as if you're not there (being able to ignore peripheral adults quickly becomes a key facet in the trainee teacher's armoury as a coping mechanism for assessment), the class' staring and pointing quickly returns to the contents of Jimmy's tissue, and your seat, already in the corner, seems to spirit itself slowly down the corridor. 'Don't mind me, I'm not really here . . . '

By far the best bet is to throw yourself into the school by getting as involved as possible. Only by working with small groups, helping out with clubs and speaking to the children can you really gauge the ethos of school, the ethos of the particular class and a true insight into your own views on teaching. If, after two weeks, you have done little more than watch a teacher teach you will only have seen a sanitized version of the profession, viewing from behind thick safety glass.

In some ways your time in school before the course even starts is as important as the time in school during the course. In perhaps as little as one or two weeks you will have to decide whether teaching is for you, what age group you want to teach and, if doing secondary, which subject. On the course you get about 20 weeks in school to answer the question of how to become a good teacher, pre-course you get just two weeks to answer 'do I want to be a teacher?'.

Although it's worth spreading yourself fairly thinly around the school, if only to ensure that the burden is evenly spread around the teachers, it's equally important to spend at least a few days with an age group you might want to teach. Prior to the course starting, I spent far more time observing Years 4 and 5 than any other classes – partly because the teachers in these year groups were particularly accommodating and partly because these seemed to be the years I would most likely end up teaching at the end of the course. Trainees are unlikely to be handed a Year 6 class – too much pressure with Standard Assessment Tasks (SATs) – and so anyone hoping to teach in upper juniors will most likely find themselves starting lower before working up.

Even if you are not sure which age group you want to teach, it is still well worth spending at least a few days concentrating on one class as this will give you a chance to get to know the pupils better and work with all the different ability groups. Teaching the gifted pupils who grasp every new concept instantly is one challenge, teaching those who need specialist help and a simplified curriculum quite another. Any experience you can get of observing both ends of the spectrum is to be grasped, especially as in any PGCE interview you will inevitably be asked about inclusion and the consequences of teaching a class with a myriad of mixed abilities. (By the way, there is no correct answer to this question; the whole profession seems divided as to whether inclusion is a good idea or not. That said, it is probably best to avoid an answer I heard on interview day when a middle-aged woman said it was better when 'the dunces were taken off to be taught elsewhere'. She didn't make it onto the course and has, no doubt, had to look for employment elsewhere, quite possibly as a *Daily Mail* columnist.)

Your time spent in school, however brief, will hopefully be enough to get you an interview or two, or at least it will once the dreaded application form has been filled in. Thankfully the human brain has an amazing ability to block out unwelcome memories and so my recollection of filling the form in is shaky. What I do recall is the standard fare of filling in qualifications, spending hours composing a covering letter that still seemed distinctly unsatisfactory and then trying to find two suitable referees, the referees having to be particularly efficient in this case as your application won't be processed until their testimonials have been submitted.

The best advice I can give is simply to get it done as quickly as possible. Universities start the interviewing process early and it's easy to miss a deadline (as I did with one of my two options). Even those that have later deadlines will still tend to start the interviewing process as soon as possible, meaning that by deadline date there can easily be thousands of applications pouring in for a mere handful of remaining places.

If your application is literate and includes reference to some time in school it should be enough to get you an interview, which is where the real battle begins. There is no shortcut to success in the interview. You will probably be there for the best part of a whole day and in that time you'll have numerous tasks and challenges to pass. They will be looking at a range of factors that will include your awareness of current educational issues, your commitment to the profession, your ability to express yourself confidently and eloquently (taking into account that some people naturally turn into jelly at interviews), your ability to both play an active, but not overbearing role in a discussion and your level of written English.

Most universities will set some form of task that requires preparation prior to the interview. In my case it was having to prepare a one-minute speech on a current educational issue. Almost everyone delivered an almost identical speech on inclusion, no doubt boring the interviewers to tears, so it's probably worth trying to think of a topic that is a bit less obvious. There's nothing worse than having to deliver a speech that sounds as if it has been plagiarized straight from the preceding candidate; instead try flicking through a recent copy of *The Times Educational Supplement* (*TES*) and finding something that really interests you. (I plumped for looking at gifted and talented pupils who, in some schools, seem to get a bum deal with all the focus of inclusion looking at the less able.)

Having planned and researched your own speech for hours I'm sure it will run perfectly, but, even if it does, don't rest on your laurels. Anyone can rehearse a good speech and so to really impress you will have to show evidence of a much wider knowledge base during any group discussion. Luckily, this does not have to be quite as hard as it sounds.

Of course, you could take what I like to call the masochist's route, spending hours reading and researching every conceivable issue, interviewing teachers past and present and perhaps touring Europe to observe educational practices abroad. You could even be really sly by finding out who your interviewers are likely to be (tutors at the university or college), reading any journals or articles they might have written and then tailoring your answers to tie in with their views. Anyone wishing to do this (and if you do, you might also want to voluntarily place yourself on the Stalkers Register) needs only to put the tutor's name into Google and browse for relevant results. Experimenting with this idea I found that, as well as writing numerous web stories, I once went to school in America and 'did disgusting things on the bus' (memories I've conveniently blacked out) and that one of my best friends is chairman of the exclusive sounding Simplewood Skateclub.

A better approach (I say this because it's the one that worked for me and so, to the best of my knowledge, has a 100 per cent success rate) is to simply read through a few copies of *the TES* and other education supplements (the *Guardian*'s is excellent) and make a few notes that strike you as being of interest. Then simply impart some of your new-found knowledge into the conversation, at times even adding a precursor such as 'as I read in *the TES* on 17 April' to sound particularly well-read. This might also serve as a useful tactic when it comes to writing the dreaded essays as it's always good to be able to throw in quotes from a range of recent publications. Equally, if you stumble across any interesting titbit on education, be it in the local rag, on the radio or down the pub, make a note of it and try to bring it out on interview day.

Academic knowledge is, of course, great, but the interviewers are not looking for teachers who are great in theory, rubbish in practice. Far more important than any reading is being able to talk about your own time in school, what you observed, what you have learnt from it and how it will affect your future practice. Hopefully you've seen a mix of good and bad practice in schools and by being able to comment on this you will show an ability to reflect critically on teaching – a key facet to both getting on and then passing the course. Being able to say what you think works in teaching is one thing, being able to back it up with examples is quite another, for instance mentioning teaching strategies and techniques that you have observed working particularly well. To this end, whenever you are in school prior to your interview you should be looking at what the teacher is actually doing, how they divide their time, how they control the class, even how they get the class out of the room quietly for assembly (or why they fail to maintain a quiet class). Make notes because, as we all know, those little gems that pop into your head pop out again just as quickly (as has happened numerous times in writing this chapter . . . ). Just don't make that note-taking too obvious. Teachers hate having assessors in, but at least the assessors have teaching experience. Having a student who has barely ever been in a classroom since leaving at 16 sat there taking copious, critical notes is probably a bit galling. The class teachers I came across were happy to impart their knowledge and answer any questions, but that's partly because I took care not to bite the hand that was feeding me.

Having spent time in school, read up on issues and planned a great speech, you should be as confident as is possible in such circumstances going into the interview. There is, though, still one more major challenge to go. Answering questions in your own, individual interview. Fortunately, teacher-training courses seem to have so far avoided going down the surreal approach favoured by some employers (what kind of fish would you be?, describe yourself only in nouns, sell yourself in personal ads style), instead choosing topics that, while somewhat mundane, at least avoid the necessity for the interviewee to imagine themselves as a contestant on a Radio 4 quiz show. Again, while there are no perfect answers there are plenty to be avoided. While waiting for my own interview I was able to earwig of my rivals, I mean potential peers (we were interviewed in a large room, I didn't put a glass to the wall), and as well as a few answers worth pinching I also heard a few gems:

Q) So, Gemma (name changed to spare Jane's blushes), why do you want to be a teacher?
A) Because you get long holidays and I came to the end of my degree not knowing what I wanted to do.

Note, also avoid 'Because I still feel like a child' and 'Because the little kiddy widdies are soooooo cutey wooty'.
Q) What experience have you had in school?
A) Tonnes, over ten years in total, although it was a fair while ago . . .
Q) Who inspired you to be a teacher and why?
A) Arnold Schwarzenegger in *Kindergarten Cop*. I admired his classroom control.
Q) What do you know about differentiation?
A) I've got loads of first-hand experience having been in the bottom class throughout school.

You're almost certain to be asked at least two of the four questions above in some form or other, so it's obviously prudent to plan skeleton answers, again working in examples you've observed in schools whenever possible.

Other questions will probably cover broad themes, unless you get a complete arse of an interviewer, so you'll need at least a passing knowledge of the National Curriculum, inclusion (catering for all pupils, including those with . . . ), special educational needs (SEN), your own qualities and why they will make you a brilliant teacher, the current issues in education (a quick read of the excellent *TES* message boards will help here), the role of teaching support and parents, your interests outside of school and, crucially, modern techniques in wiping vomit from carpets (and, before I forget, there is no better technique than putting wet sand onto the deposit, allowing it to dry and then vacuuming it up).

Pre-course, there is nothing to catch you out, no curve balls thrown. As an American motivational speaker might say 'success comes from within'. Spend time in schools, keep your eyes open and do plenty of research and there is every chance that you'll find yourself on the course. And if you don't there is no need to despair. Try to think about where you went wrong and, if possible, apply again the following year having built up your school experience. Your commitment will be testament to your suitability as the course is full of ups and downs. A small down before it starts only serves to put you on a bigger high once you do earn a place.

# 4 Death by paperwork

It sounded like the easiest of tasks. 'Make sure you read through all the school's health and safety literature on your second visit', said the handy little note on page 74 of Appendix 9b in Course Handbook C. It looked like it was turning into the 13th labour of Hercules. My school's health and safety document makes *War and Peace* look like the hasty scribblings of a failing GCSE student. It has two pages on dealing with rabies, three pages given over to avalanches (seemingly a major problem in Cheshire) and a mini section devoted to baking with kilns. To say it is definitive would be like saying Elizabeth Taylor likes toasters. Getting the 10 kilogram document down from its precarious perch 3 metres up, surely a health and safety issue in itself, and then reading it was not a task to fill me with great enthusiasm. Fortunately, help was at hand.

A fellow student, a disconcertingly organized one at that, was also after the document. With that bright-eyed and bushytailed keenness of youth, the type that makes you view the humble NUS card as the key to a brave new world, and Freshers' Week as the height of 1960s style hedonism, he was up on a chair in a flash, whisking the folder away in the next. 'Excuse me', I ventured after him, 'I'll be needing a look at that as well.' His reply was blissful. 'Don't worry mate, I'm going to read it all and then I can tell you the key bits.' Heaven!

But I don't mean to give the impression that being relieved of health and safety pressure merely freed me up to watch *Countdown* (though it did); it also gave me valuable planning time. Next week we are in our schools all week and I have resolved to take the bull by the horns, to step onto the plate and to do all those other clichés that used to be scattered so liberally in my sports copy. All being well, I will deliver parts of the literacy and numeracy lessons and also help out with science and ICT. For numeracy, the focus of my thinking at present as tomorrow we have a mental arithmetic test, the lesson will be kept simple – perhaps just simple additions and subtractions involving dice and counting blocks. Literacy could involve a simplified version of *Countdown*, that way I can claim this afternoon as research time. Three, four or five letters put on the board so that the class can then try to make a word of any length out of them. The more able could perhaps write a four-letter word, while others might manage one of two letters, thus building in the differentiation for abilities that is vital in all primary lessons.

Of course there's a chance that all those plans will go flying out of the window should the class choose to play up for their new teacher, especially as my behaviour management skills are some-what untested, but I do have a couple of aces up my sleeve.

Firstly, the class teacher has promised to go for a little walk with some of the more disruptive elements during my first few lessons and, secondly, there's nothing that a bit of bribery can't achieve. The class are carrying out topic work on Australia and, knowing a man with a didgeridoo (a long story . . . ), I'm hoping to get a treat lined up for them. The thought of seeing it, let alone missing out on hearing it played, will hopefully ensure good behaviour and, if they are really good, we might even have a go at making our own. However, it will have to be from a kitchen role tube as models, for hygiene reasons, cannot be made from toilet roll tubes. Page 247 of the Health and Safety Manual taught me that. Page 248 taught me that computers should not be used near sinks.

# 5 Strictly need-to-know

Last week I wrote that my behaviour management skills were untested. This week I can report that they have had a good run out, and failed miserably.

It happened during a literacy lesson. I can't really blame the class – the lesson was so dull that even I was getting restless – but still it came as a surprise. It had all been going so well before. The class happily called me Mr Carbooty, or Mr Barboobie, they told me what they did the night before and they listened intently while I read them their afternoon story. I even thought that I had developed a tactic for dealing with any mini uprising: stop talking, tell the class that if they didn't quieten down I would have to stop, listen to the hush descend and then start again. When reading *Wolfie at the Door* it worked a treat, the class needed to know whether Wolfie was going to eat the house's huddled inhabitants. When explaining the Grapheme pattern of peep (p-ee-p) it didn't. Evidently 5-year-olds can take or leave English language theory.

Still, I won't be beaten that easily, so tomorrow it's back into the lion's den. Starters will be a lesson on the -at ending, words like cat, fat, bat and a few rude ones. The main course will be a science lesson on the senses and, in particular, taste. On a side note, I've now realized how being a teacher will impinge on all areas of my life – even this afternoon I found myself queuing at the supermarket with a basket full of bizarre fruits. For the benefit of the elderly lady in the queue, I'd like to use this juncture to point out that the fruits were bought to act as a taste test and not, as I fear she thought judging by the looks she was giving me, as the saccharine basis of an adult game. Not that I should bother explaining myself as given her attempts at extracting two pences from her tiny purse, a process akin to a crab picking up ice cubes, it's pretty unlikely that she'll be finding herself flicking through these pages anytime soon.

But I digress, I was talking about my expensive science lesson. Expensive because it's that time of year that student scroungers everywhere know as free money. A teacher's training salary on top of a student loan means that the kids get mangoes, pineapples and caviar when before they'd have got value baked beans and been told how lucky they were. Of course, not all money will go on the class – Thursday night is 2-for-1 night at the all you can eat curry house and so I'll be treating my girlfriend to a night out for what she'd have you believe was the first time in four years. True or not, it might be the last night out for four years as I've been told repeatedly in the last week that teaching will take over my whole life. One person has even told me that student teachers shouldn't have any sort of life outside of teaching as there is so much to be learnt.

It's a sobering thought, and as such it's a thought that I'll ignore. I already know how tough the planning is going to be – I've been dealing with a double dose of it for the past few weeks. When not planning bits of lessons I've been putting the final touches to wedding preparations (my own, I'm not sadistic enough to try arranging someone else's wedding) and when not ringing caterers or chasing up relatives I've been reading through policy documents. I'd put this weekend aside for planning, forgetting that my stag do was pencilled in. I have a sneaking feeling I won't get much work down while sellotaped to the Boeing 737 from Manchester to Beijing.

And so for once I've been forced to change the habit of a life-time by finishing work months rather than minutes before the final deadline. This week I've knocked off a couple of essays due for December and, thanks to the budget bumper book of wedding speeches (bought before the loan went in . . . ), my wedding speech is pretty much done.

One thing still worries me though. With so much to do, it's easy to get a bit muddled and I have visions of standing in front of a packed dinner hall on October 30th and reading a wedding speech that begins 'today children, we will be dancing in the style of a shadow puppet', while on my mentor's desk in school will be a few scribbled notes saying how happy I am to be spending the rest of my life with her. And she thought she only had to put up with me for seven more weeks . . .

# 6 I'm going to die

So much for teaching being the easy life. My dreams of six-week summer holidays, trips to the Natural History Museum, a bonus card at BHS and a 20-year stint in a sleepy Lakeland village were all put in perspective this week by the news that I've signed up to an early grave.

Sorry if that sounds melodramatic, but I'm only passing on what a lecturer said in one of the most demotivating motivational speeches of all time. Oh yes, the blood and thunder of a First World War general barking 'go over the top for king and country' has nothing on this guy.

Teaching is a killer. If the kids don't get you (and they probably won't – this isn't America), the stress will. Not while you're teaching, though. Instead, by a cruel irony, the accumulation suddenly hits home on retirement. The average life expectancy for a teacher retiring aged 65 is just 18 months. No wonder they still have the offer of final salary pension schemes – it's not like they are going to be around to cash it in.

Whether the stat is true is anyone's guess, 64 per cent of statisticians are liars after all, what is undeniable is that teaching is a stressful profession with those extended holidays often the only thing stopping a complete nervous breakdown. Already I have heard horror stories that would seem unbelievable in any other profession. There was the teacher who turned up for work one day, found himself unable to get out of his car due to fear of what the day would hold, and drove off never to be seen again. Then there are the teachers whose reason for disappearing at breaks is because they need to hide somewhere – either for a sob, or to take a few swigs of their favourite nerve-calmer. Some teachers are on long-term sick leave due to stress, others have simply walked out to join the dole queue. Anyone who thinks that teaching is an easy job is mistaken. Anyone coming out with the old adage 'those who can do, those who can't teach', is a fool. A more accurate take might be 'those who can do, those who can't need a teacher'.

But to be forewarned is to be forearmed, and so I don't intend to accept meekly an early invite to meet my maker. The two big contributing factors to a teacher's stress levels are the constant paperwork and planning and also the children's behaviour. To get on top of the planning, my scheme is straightforward. Get myself organized, keep everything in a neat format that makes it easily searchable and then, when I get to 45, move to a village with only seven children, that way cutting down on paperwork immeasurably.

Controlling behaviour will be more of a problem, especially as I have realized that I am not actually a natural in this field, I was merely enjoying a honeymoon period with the class as they sussed me out. It didn't take them very long either and I fear that they now see me as a soft touch that won't follow his threats through. Something will have to be done about that, an example needs to be set. Someone might have to lose a whole housepoint.

Today, though, I was giving them out, especially to the group I taught literacy to. For the first time, I got to take a complete literacy lesson from start to finish, albeit for a small group, and, if I do say so myself, the results were pretty good. The children hit their learning objectives and, as a teacher, you can't ask for much more than that, not that I should crow as it doesn't happen too often. Next week I'll be taking another group in literacy and numeracy. The literacy lesson will focus on an exciting children's story, the numeracy will be based on basic additions. It's not hard to tell which will grab the class' attention more readily. Numeracy for kids has always been a killer – drab lessons teaching a subject that needs a bit of magic to bring it to life. And that, I have decided, should be my aim – to make my lessons interesting. It might just prove to be a life-extending strategy as I reckon it's not the stress or the planning that kills off teachers – it's the being exposed to 10,000 dull maths lessons.

# 7 No, no, please, not the housepoints

What is it about housepoints that makes them so magical to children? Take a misbehaving class – shouting will have no effect, threats of losing play time go unheard and polite requests are scoffed by even the most mild mannered of five years, but threaten to remove a housepoint and suddenly the only sound to be heard is that of faint, muffled sobs. There are some exceptions, the class wriggler high on cheap orange squash and the aloof protégé James Dean to name but two, these though are rare exceptions. On the whole, housepoints work where all manner of other threats fail.

It matters not that the child threatened with the loss might be bottom of the housepoint table already. The fact that they already have absolutely no hope of winning any sort of prize for their pitiful weekly haul goes unnoticed. Often the loss only succeeds in taking them from minus seven to minus eight, a mere 248 behind the leader, however while there is still that faint hope of picking up 300 housepoints for a piece of scribbled work late on Friday afternoon they stay hopeful. 'Oh Mr Carbooty, anything but the housepoints.'

Given their widespread usage and undoubted effectiveness you might be surprised to learn that I am already sick of the system. My problem is that far from acting as a reward for good behaviour, they merely act as a deterrent for bad. Each week, the same two or three children compete at the top of the table for a prize, which then carries on for bigger and better monthly and termly awards. The system is horribly self-fulfilling. Little Johnny shines in the first term of Year 1, Little Johnny wins prize after prize, Little Johnny quickly grows to love the system, the teachers note Little Johnny as a model of behaviour and are always on-hand to witness his latest accomplishment, Little Johnny sails through school with a love of learning that will take him far. Meanwhile, Bobby takes time to settle in school, has a couple of early run-ins with his teacher, fails to pick up housepoints, gets noted as 'awkward' and leaves school another soul lost to the system.

Along the line, Bobby will have put plenty of effort into his work, produced pieces to be genuinely proud of and spent many hours hoping against hope that he'd be that week's winner. However, his individual pieces of work will have gone almost entirely unrewarded, save for a few housepoints here and there which ultimately proved completely irrelevant.

The system, or at least the system as I have seen it applied, is also far too arbitrary. Housepoints are given out like Bibles at a Gideon giveaway at the start of the week, merely to act as the ballast to be offloaded later in the week. There is also a horrible randomness whereby five housepoints can be given for jumping off a bench in PE and yet only one for having spent 17 hours on *Encarta* over the weekend researching the natural habitat of the lesser-spotted Toucan.

Children are given rewards for things they should be doing as a matter of course – walking down the corridor, holding doors open, stopping fighting – building a natural sense that they should act for reward and not merely because it's right to behave in a certain manner. Groups are rewarded en masse merely on the basis of which house they are in – the naughtiest pupil in the winning house might get an extra five minutes play time, the best behaved in another house will get nothing. It is as unfair and divisive as the old strategy of 'I'm keeping you all in until the culprit owns up.'

Anyway, rant over, though I'm not really sure where it came from. Perhaps it can be put down to my other major complaint at the moment – illness. Nothing serious, just an ongoing cold (brought about by being in close proximity to 30 other colds) that makes it feel as if I'm downing half a pint of egg-nog and two liquidized eels every time I swallow. Children (and I can't understand why I don't remember this from my youth) are always ill. Even when they're not properly ill, they're ill, with the coughing and the sneezing, the wheezing and the spluttering, the hiccuping and the rumblings. All this, albeit very roundaboutly, leads me to an idea. Something is forming in the back of my brain whereby children are rewarded by being given Tunes to suck – thus alleviating their cold and diminishing their ability to make noise all in one go. Undoubtedly there are flaws in this plan – the rotting of teeth, the annoyance of sweets being crunched en masse, the fact that, as plans go, it is completely useless, but none of these things bother me at present. In my flu-addled stupor (I'm a man, so the common cold has become flu in the space of 200 words) I've even decided to turn it into a book. *Singing to your Tune*, it will be called. Expect to read the first extracts at some point in the dim and distant future . . .

# 8  Yin vs yang: the sequel

Having left work to rediscover life as a student on a teacher-training course, I have found myself veering between student life and working life during the past few weeks. Both, it has to be said, come naturally. My yin side remembers student life – recoiling from just six hours of lectures per week if it means missing a *Jerry Springer* omnibus. My yang side harks back to working life and the daily lung-busting sprint for the 7.02 train, mobile in hand in case I should miss it and have to ring up with an implausible excuse for being late.

Naturally, as in a mediocre (is there any other sort?) Jean Claude Van Damme film, my yin and yang have generally been at war. My good part wants to settle down to eight hours of study, my evil half (I call it Aikio) wanting nothing more than a beer, a curry and comfy spot on the sofa to watch Major League Baseball live.

Generally, it has not been too much of a fight. My good half takes after me – 11 stones of malleability and Lilly-liveredness – leaving Akio, a ninth Dan black belt, free to have his wicked way. This week, perhaps uniquely, my yin and yang have resembled an advert for natural yoghurt, realigning themselves in perfect harmony.

What, you might ask, have I done to achieve such a spiritual balance? Have I started Yogic flying, read the Koran backwards, taken up a voluntary job with the Samaritans or started humming the complete works of Cat Stevens? Sadly, the answer is none of the above. Instead the aligning of yin and yang has been achieved entirely by circumstances outside of my control.

For this week it has not been a contradiction in terms to be a student teacher. Teachers have the week off for half term, students have the week off for reading, and so student teachers have the week off to read about teaching. Or at least they should have. Sadly, and from talking to my peers I am not alone in this, I have found it nigh on impossible to settle down to anything even approaching hard work during the past few days. Fair enough, I knocked out a science essay on Monday, critically analysing how questions are used to enhance lessons, and Tuesday also saw me busy as my teaching studies assignment with 1,200 words on creating a positive learning environment, whistled onto the screen, entirely missing out the usual, to be recommended, draft stage. However, those two are just the tip of the iceberg. There's still ICT, maths and another science project to be done and if that's not enough I have a sneaky feeling that neither completed essay is actually all that good.

But as a teacher it is essential to be analytical and so the question I should be asking is why have I found it so hard to knuckle down? The main reason, and quite a good one if you ask me, must be my forthcoming nuptials. Saturday sees me tie the knot and although I am not particularly nervous about the day itself, I have found much of my time taken up with playing with the ever-increasing pile of goodies delivered to our door courtesy of Debenhams Direct (I am slurping on an improbable grapefruit and raspberry ice cream smoothie even as I write . . . ).

To be honest, though, it all seems a bit surreal that I will be married in three days time and if it wasn't for the ever-increasing pile of stainless-steel small electricals I might well believe I had dreamt the whole thing. Of course, I can't wait for it to happen, but it's what comes after that bothers me (no, not that bit, all you of dirty minds!). Next week I'm back in school for the second week of my placement and, unlike the first week, I have got precious little prepared – partly because there is little that can be prepared until I have seen the teacher's plans and partly because I have had other, more pressing, things on my mind.

But now is not the time to worry about next week in school. I'm sure you'll agree that other things must take precedence at present. Saturday will fly by, Sunday will be spent recovering and then on Monday I'll be in school, perhaps earning a few brownie points for foregoing a honeymoon in favour of a 100 per cent course-attendance record. All romantics should fear not, though. Mrs Barbuti-to-be (as she loves being called) will get her honeymoon after all, just not straight away. Figuring that the only holidays on offer in November were either last-minute deals to Crete or coach packages to Blackpool, we decided to change tack and go skiing. Come December we'll jet off to Austria for a week of snow ploughs, broken bones and après-ski. Teaching, though, will never be far from my mind. 'How can I turn my experiences into a lesson?' 'What are the different forces in action when doing a snow plough?' 'If a mountain is 5,897 metres how many feet is it?'

Actually, that was a blatant lie. I love the course, but at present teaching couldn't be further from my mind. For now the rigours of planning, assessment and monitoring can wait – I've got a suit to try on.

# 9  First placement

If you don't have a few nerves going into your first placement, you're not normal. You might be on Prozac, you might not actually care about teaching or you might be an android. Whichever it is, you will be in a very small minority.

When I started my first placement my stomach was tight, my hands sweaty and my witty repartee replaced by stammering nonsense. You are being thrust into an alien environment full of new people and faces whose names you'll have to try to remember from a five-second introduction, shown round a sprawling building full of corridors and identikit classrooms, and finally deposited into the hands of a class teacher who has got plenty of other things to be bothering about without your intrusion. In my case, this initial introduction was slightly more nerve-racking as, despite setting off with time to spare, I got caught in a convoluted one-way system and arrived, at high speed, with a minute to spare.

The first day of your placement is very much like the first day at a new job. With the teacher and class busy, it can be hard to make any sort of impression or to feel like you have been anything other than a spare part. At least in a new job, though, you will be given responsibility and will gradually get to be held in higher esteem – they have paid for you after all and have chosen you over other candidates so they must want you there. With placements, there are no such assurances. You might have been thrust on the school and thrust on the teacher. However hard you try to fit in and make a positive impression it is possible that there will always be an underlying air that, while someone to be put up with, you are not someone to be actively welcomed.

This might sound like a horrible situation to be in, but it really needn't be. Although terribly clichéd, it is a truism to say that you are not there to make friends. Instead you have to make sure that you get what you want and need from the first placement. If you find the school welcoming that is a bonus, possibly even one that will lead to future employment. If they aren't welcoming take it on the chin and think about how you will make it easier for student teachers when you're teaching, because it can be guaranteed that, if you teach for any length of time, you will have a trainee to nurture at some stage.

Initially you will get to know your class through a series of day visits. These are a wonderful opportunity to get to know your class and settle into school with a minimum of pressure. This time also enables you to learn the pupils' names, a task I found manageable only after drawing a map of the classroom and writing their names by where they sat. (This method worked perfectly until, under the guise of Mind Friendly Learning, the whole classroom at my second school was reorganized so that the class got used to working with different partners. One thing I learnt from this was that nine-year-old boys really don't like being addressed by the wrong name. Especially if it's Gemma.)

One of the biggest mistakes I made during these initial visits was in becoming over-friendly with the class. When your work is limited to overseeing groups, taking pupils for individual reading and making up numbers in playground games of football, it is hard to establish yourself as a potential teacher. I found that the class saw me more as an occasional help, similar to a parent helper, than as a teacher. This was fine at first, when I was just reading them stories or taking the very occasional lesson, but later on it made it very difficult to administer reprimands to children who saw me more as a friend than a teacher.

It's also worth using the initial visits constructively. The first day in school can probably be put down to acclimatization and settling in, after that it's time to get busy. Folders, the bane of the trainee teacher's life, have to be bought and then filled with thousands of pieces of redundant paperwork. All the school policies go in first, with pertinent points highlighted to prove that you haven't just stuck it in wholesale without reading it (as if you would even consider doing such a thing). The Ofsted report, or bits of it at least, also goes in, as does a full class list, class and school timetables, list of resources, details on any pupils with special educational needs, list of helpers for the class and pretty much any other background information you can come across. In most walks of life the adage 'quality not quantity' rings true; in teacher training, at least where files are concerned, it's the opposite.

The final thing to consider, and something I wish had popped into my head earlier than six weeks into the placement, is getting around other classes. Your own class teacher, contrary to any protestations they may make (mine didn't), will be more than happy to have you out from under their feet for a few hours and the other teachers will no doubt be delighted to take you. This is especially useful if you find yourself on a course that insists on giving you placements in different Key Stages even if you are entirely certain which age group you want to teach.

My first placement was with a Year 1 class, sweet but as far away from the age range I wanted to teach as was possible and so I found much of the time irrelevant as I knew that I had no desire to end up teaching basic counting skills, the letters of the alphabet or how to tie shoelaces. But by observing other teachers, even just for the odd lesson, you can learn an amazing amount. You can compare teaching styles, seeing what works and what doesn't by direct comparison, see how techniques are adapted for teaching different age groups and also start getting an overview of how the curriculum progresses as pupils move up the school.

It might also help remove a few preconceptions. Although I was pretty sure that I wanted to teach Year 6 it became apparent that Year 4 or 5 might be a nicer starting point, none of that nasty SATs pressure or jealous glances from colleagues who had been hankering after Year 6 for years. I learnt this by spending time in the different classes and comparing what the job was like. Year 6 is undeniably a superb challenge, one I would like in the future, but the stress of SATs is immense and as an NQT there's more than enough to worry about already.

As the first placement goes on, with weeks spent in school instead of days, the focus changes from learning about the school and its practices to developing your own teaching. The first few lessons won't be perfect – if they are you are in a very happy position whereby you have very little to learn on the course – so it is important to be able to take positives out of them. Even if you spend twice as long as you should on the starter session, watching in horror as the classroom turns into a riot zone and failing to achieve any of the hoped-for learning objectives, the lesson can still be used as a positive, something to move forward from.

The key is to analyse the lesson, identifying where it went right and wrong and, from this, to draw out a couple of areas which can be improved. The areas that you choose to focus on should be big ones, ones that are crucial to your development as a teacher. There is no point focusing on improving the plenary if you cannot keep control of the class.

Just being aware of a problem won't actually eradicate it. The key to teaching, or indeed any profession, is to spend time developing your own practice and working out how it will develop. In teaching this means you will have to do a bit of wider reading to find theoretical ways of improving your practice, talk to your tutors who will be able to give you some more down-to-earth advice and find out what other people on the course are doing.

Most importantly of all, you will need to actually make the changes, however unnatural they may feel. One tip I was taught was to raise my hand whenever there was unwanted noise in the class and then wait for everyone else to shut-up and put their hand up. Frankly, this felt ridiculous at first and it also failed to work as I did it half-heartedly, almost apologetically, and most of the class failed to even notice. Actually, they probably did notice, they just ignored me. The 'hands up' strategy only worked when I did it confidently, puffing out my chest, raising my arm and giving a few withering glances as necessary. And, when it started working, it was wonderful – an easy way of keeping classroom control and a problem area that could be ticked off allowing me to move on to something else.

Probably the key to the first placement is making sure that, by the end of it, you feel in a position whereby going into your second placement you can teach at least reasonably effective lessons. The first placement is where you take a great big wadge of sandpaper to your practice, getting rid of massive splintered edges. The second placement is where you apply the polish.

In your first placement you should also start getting standards ticked off. Standards would be the bane of the trainee's life, if I hadn't already awarded that dubious honour to files, and are worthy of their own chapter. Which is exactly what they'll get (see Chapter 19). In placement one, you should try to get as many ticked off as possible, again easing the pressure going into your second placement. A couple of the standards I worried about overtly at this stage were concerned with adding to the overall life of the school (basically helping out with clubs) and dealing (not the official word) with parents.

Adding to the life of the school is fairly straightforward as teachers will generally be delighted to have an extra helper at after-school clubs and will merrily tick the standard off. The whole topic of how many hours you should spend in school each day, however, is something of a grey area. On my first day, I was merrily told that I should be in at 8.30am each morning and was not to leave before 4.30pm. This meant that there were days, especially early on when I wasn't teaching much, where I was left virtually kicking my heels in school waiting for 4.30pm to roll around (what made it far more annoying was that the vagaries of the rail system meant that I arrived at school at 7.30am and then had no train home until after 6pm . . . ). I'd advise any trainee that, while they need to look keen, there is no point overdoing it by staying at school into the early evening, especially if it's at the expense of planning or reflection that would be better carried out at home. The school is not your employer and so there is absolutely no need to go to all the staff meetings or other gatherings – only go to get some experience of what they are like (I found the staff meetings I attended to be very much like negotiations between Iran and Iraq).

As for parents, well you shouldn't have to worry about them too much in your first placement. They'll just be those people at the school gate who talk about their children's 'new teacher' behind your back without making any effort to introduce themselves. I tended to become two-dimensional when parents came into the classroom at the start of the day, especially early on in the placement, fading into the paintwork. This was partly through nerves and partly because answering the same question 'so who are you?' 32 times can become a tad tiring.

All those little things – parents, staff meetings, governors, interviews and other stresses – are for the future. Placement one is all about settling in, settling into school life, settling into teaching and settling into the course.

You need to work hard and be observant, but perhaps most of all you need to be realistic. If you have things to work on, and you will, then work on them and don't bury your head in the sand thinking it will come right naturally. That is what the assessor will want to see when they come in to observe you teaching a lesson, your ability to reflect on your own practice and take pointers on board. When I was assessed, I was naturally nervous. Here was someone coming in to watch me teach and they had the power to either class me as satisfactory or at risk. Being classed as satisfactory would mean just that, obviously. You were developing reasonably and could be left alone by the assessor until their final report, in the final week of the placement. A tick in the 'at risk' box means that you're going to see a lot more of the assessor. Once a week they'll pull up in their Ford Mondeo, clipboard in hand, ready to deliver their verdict on your teaching. But, although they may look a bit like the Demon Headmaster, they really aren't all that fearful. They just want to see some progress so that they can tick you off as ok and save themselves a raft of paperwork.

Whether satisfactory or at risk, you'll get a wealth of advice and things to work on from the assessor and, when they come back to write the final report (at which point they won't normally ask to see you teach again, they merely want a chat), they'll want to see evidence that you weren't asleep when they gave you those snippets of experience.

They will also want to see that your folders are in decent order so it's well worth stocking up on dividers and highlighters and making sure that all your lesson plans are easily accessible. When starting your course, you will be given a handbook that includes, amongst an amazing amount of what can be best classed as 'filler material', a guide to keeping your files in good order. Stick this in at the front of your files, follow it religiously and you can't go too far wrong – I say this as someone who failed to do this initially and thus found myself enjoying 3am sessions filling in the blanks the day before being assessed.

Whatever happens, though, don't get too stressed and try to enjoy your time in school. It is worth remembering that this is just the introduction and, in the long run, doesn't really matter all that much. Stress will come in the form of lessons going wrong and also from the assessor, but these are fleeting moments in what should be a fascinating period of weeks. As a trainee you're at the start of a long journey, and in your first placement you've barely taken a couple of steps. The real stress comes in placement two . . .

# 10  Coming out fighting

The chance to attend a staff meeting on changes to assessment procedures – coming just hours after my wedding it sounded far too
much fun to turn down, and so it proved. Tired and emotional,
with vows of love, understanding and friendship still ringing in my
ears, I entered the cauldron, eyeing the protagonists with chests
puffed out, battle lines drawn up, honour to be defended.

The meeting had been brought forward, last half term's time of
4pm changed to 3.45, when it should have been moved back. Way
back. A 10pm watershed might have been more appropriate. The
early start was meant to facilitate an early exit, but anyone hoping
to be home in time for the *Weakest Link* was in for a disappointment. Cups of tea and cakes – the staples of a school's staffroom –
were for once missing, not to save time, merely so that battle could
commence that bit sooner (and so that when it did there weren't
missiles readily at hand).

First, though, the formalities. Assembly rotas to be decided,
bonfire night planned, the Elgar-thon (a charity event that, in this
school at least, seems to have taken precedence over Children in
Need) rearranged. And then, as the meeting's scribe picked up his
weapon of choice, the two main pugilists settled into their cushions
and started dropping their aural bombs.

From the purple corner, the literacy coordinator tried explaining the changes to assessing speaking and listening while doing very
little of the latter. A challenge came from the turquoise camp – her
system, she claimed, was working perfectly. She had done it for five
years, results were improving, it was quick and efficient and even
saved the school a small fortune on black ink. 'But everyone else is
using sheet 73247 pt B, section 64', came the coordinator's reply.
The silence and puzzled mutterings from the rest of the staffroom
suggested otherwise – it seemed everyone had their own system,

everyone thought theirs was best, even the system that seemed to consist of making no assessment whatsoever, by far the easiest to maintain, though with obvious disadvantages elsewhere.

The debate raged on. Twenty minutes with no resolution at hand – a motion was passed to debate the subject again at a later date when camps would be further entrenched. That meeting is scheduled to last a month, Kofi Annan has been called in to keep the peace.

With no chance to even start debating how to assess the children's writing, the argument did a neat flip and hunter became hunted, hunted became – well you get the idea. Assessing RE was next on the agenda. Previously, RE had escaped becoming part of the Government's drive to turn every single tree into another stack of meaningless, bureaucratic paperwork, but that's all about to change. Soon, the coordinator told a hushed staffroom, there will have to be six assessments a year, the announcement coming to whatever is the exact opposite of a ticker-tape parade amidst gasps of sheer ecstasy. What on earth should be done with these assessments was left as a mute point – why we should be collecting data on whether five-year-olds can tell you the central facets of Christianity, or any other faith for that matter, is beyond me. I guess it is because assessment is king at present. The odd token gesture to reduce the burden might be made – SATs possibly ending at Key Stage 1 being a perfect example – but such moves only clear the way for even more assessment to come in via the back door.

If it's not enough that RE is now assessed, it now seems that even art must conform to the same standards. A class of 30 six-year-olds might make prints using leafs as a stencil – the result 30 pictures that, if not pretty much identical, at least share striking resemblances. These pictures, these congruent constructions, must be graded – an above average, average and below average example sent off somewhere, probably to a Postal Box in London – as the data for some study or other. Grading the region's leaf-printing skills compared to the rest of Europe, using the colour schemes to produce a complete psychological analysis of the unsuspecting child – who knows how any of these figures are used, or indeed whether they are actually used at all, save to light a very large fire somewhere. Already I can see the stress of constant assessment. I like to think that the staffroom argument between two motherly, mild-mannered, members of staff wasn't really a sign of any deep-seated dislike, more a sign that all teachers are under enough stress to carry out the existing assessments while staying on top of the teaching framework.

Perhaps under those circumstances the Government should start looking at ways to get them back to what they love doing – teaching – and away from pointless pen-pushing. It seems to me that that is the only way to reinvigorate learning and also the only way to stop thousands of otherwise placid teachers turning into regular Rocky Marcianos every time the dreaded A bomb is dropped.

# 11 Standards swap shop

There's something about the term 'student essay' that brings about a horrible sense of foreboding in me. It's not the words, endless conjunctions, quotes and waffling paragraphs combined with a large font size can make any piece of writing appear 2,000 words. Nor is it the marking – at least not until essay return day. Instead, it's the horrible memory of late-night writing, 4am sessions spent huddled over a pile of books, notepad and a cup of viscous coffee, the silence only punctuated by the antics of my digs' own Casanova.

I'd hoped that it would be different this time, that five years in work might have instilled a certain responsibility in me. Instead, it seems the old cliché is true – you really can't teach an old (actually, I prefer non-young) dog new tricks.

This wouldn't be a problem if the PGCE teacher-training course was anything like my degree – periods of rest punctuated by periods in the pub, punctuated by the occasional, inconsiderately timetabled lecture. As I have found, and am finding even in writing this chapter (naturally, done at the last minute), it is far more of a problem when those essays are due in on Monday and Tuesday and then Wednesday – which by rights should be a day of rest, or half-day working at worst – is spent in school. A 6.40am sprint for the train followed by eight hours of gruelling classroom management. But I should stop moaning, I only have myself to blame for leaving things to the last minute. And also I have started to notice that I'm sounding like an old codger – the type of man who would grow cacti in his garden just to ensure any ball kicked over the fence would be sure to puncture. However, I have not mentioned my essay-writing slackness just to moan, nor just as a lengthy intro to take me some way towards my allotted word count. I have mentioned it because my attitude towards essays is in stark contrast to my attitude towards planning.

My sole aim on the course is to come out the other end as well-prepared for a full-time teaching role as possible, and with that aim in mind it has become easy to prioritize. When, on a Friday evening, I find myself with the choice of either researching for an essay or planning an engaging numeracy lesson for a class of 30 five-year-olds it will always be the essay that is allowed to slip. There can be no debate – write a poor essay and at worst you have let yourself down; plan a poor lesson, or series of lessons, and you let 30 children down and potentially hamper their progress.

The time in school will also, ultimately, be far more important to our own development on the course. The essays have to be passed, but what really matters are our PDR files – a record showing that we have hit the necessary standards and are ready to be put in front of a class unaided by man or beast. At first the PDR file appears daunting, there are 30-odd standards to be hit (I haven't counted them all, it got too depressing at 32) and if just one is missed it's bye bye to a teaching career, for the time being at least. On closer inspection, though, most are pretty straightforward and it's probably fair to say that if you can't hit most of them you don't have any place in a classroom, or at least not on the teaching side of the desk. Of course I won't bore you with all of them, I'll save that for a chapter where I'm really struggling for words, but a few examples of the standards are that you have to have high expectations of the pupils; you have to differentiate lessons for different abilities; and you have to make good use of resources in teaching.

Already, people are starting to get the standards ticked off and that's before the first big placement, a three-week block that starts on Monday. Towards the end there will be a few boxes left unticked, with students desperately trying to plan a lesson that sees their remaining standards crossed off the list. I'm hoping to hit the standards with at least enough breathing space to avoid a mad panic some time around next May, but just in case I don't I have been devising a contingency plan. My first idea came after watching a re-run of *Saturday Morning Swap Shop* (oddly enough on a Wednesday evening on cable channel 837). Why not swap standards? If people need standards, but have hit others more than once, then they could start trading to get a full set – it would be like Panini sticker albums, only without the annoyance of getting a pack containing six Gary Mabbutts. Like sticker albums, though, the plan won't work as they'll be one elusive standard that every-one is missing.

Far easier would be trading in cold-hard cash, but I'd like to avoid being involved in a scandal involving bribing a teacher – it could jeopardize my career somewhat. A far better idea will be just to knuckle down to hard work, put in some good planning and make sure I leave no room for doubting that I have hit the standards. With that in mind, I'm off to do some more planning, in fact I'm so keen to get on that I won't even have time to finish this sente.

# 12  Flu, vomit and Noel Edmonds

Fans of *Monty Python* will remember a famous scene in *The Meaning of Life* when an obese gentleman – Mr Creosote I believe – liberally vomits over the clientèle of a posh restaurant after eating one 'waffer thin mint' too many. Younger comedy buffs will also be all too aware of the art of comedic chundering from the current series of *Little Britain*. It is putrid, it's puerile, but it is also quite funny. Indeed some television celebrities have made an entire career out of covering guests in fake sick (Noel Edmonds, Keith Chegwin – I'm thinking of you).

However, while we can all agree that a technicoloured yawn on television will always raise a brief chuckle, my humour banks run dry when it comes to sick in the classroom. Prior to this week, I can honestly say that I had never seen anyone be sick in the classroom. In my old Grammar School losing control of one's oesophagus was frowned upon, so imagine my surprise this week (and it's only Wednesday) at having to clear up three separate little deposits.

Sadly there is not time to go into minute detail about the three incidents, suffice it to say that for all three it went something like: girl comes in looking white as a sheet, girl struggles through a literacy lesson that leaves several others looking white, girl is sick, trainee teacher rushes for sand, girl goes home with mum. I'm expecting more of the same on Thursday and Friday. I'm even running a little book on it and offer odds of 2/1 against more than five being ill this week – I doubt even BetFred are that generous.

I bring this up (sorry) not to ask for sympathy at having to clear up vomit (in any case all I do is throw a bit of sand over the sick – it's the caretaker, and the mother, of course, who have the really hard cleaning job). No, I mention it just as anecdotal evidence of the level of sickness rife in our nation's schools. In a class of around 30 pupils, there have been as many as seven off at any one time this week and

I doubt that more than half have been in all three days this week. Some of these children are obviously in need of a few days off – and the flip side is that there is nothing worse than an ill child coming in as they can be sure to make at least another five ill – but others, judging by their ability to attend their friends' birthday parties and apparently eat copious quantities of chicken nuggets, could probably struggle in.

All this sickness naturally has a knock-on effect to the teachers. The seasoned pros seem to carry on regardless, they're probably immune to any illness by now and could spend a month camping naked in Borneo without need for jabs. The rest of us, including the humble trainee, seem to wear the weary look of someone liable to keel over at any moment. For the past two days I have had aches in places I didn't know existed, had tissues plugged up my nose to stop the constant running and have been in bed by 7pm sharp with a hot water bottle and cup of cocoa. Today, I went a step further and bought some extra-strength painkillers from the zoo. The result – absolute bliss, a trance-like state normally only experienced by ravers at an Orbital gig.

And so at present, schools up and down Britain resemble a deleted scene from *Dawn of the Dead*, with mucus-filled kids wandering behind semi-dazed teachers. Actually, they don't at all. I'm just feeling sorry for myself because I'm suffering the occupational hazard of going down with the flu. Still, at least I have plenty to look forward to, and I don't just mean a belated honeymoon to Austria. Next week we have a touring drama production coming to school to give a performance in the style of an American chat show. Already my mind is being drawn to images of Legs Akimbo in Royston Vasey. It should be a hoot.

# 13  The Apes of Wrath

If I remember correctly (and there's a fair chance that I don't, given that the other day I spent the first 30 minutes after waking convinced I worked in a chocolate mousse factory), last week I mentioned something about a touring drama company coming to school. With 700 words to write and no other topic immediately springing to mind, I suppose I should write something about that little episode.

The drama, based on bullying and featuring one chirpy young man and two chirpy young women running around and waving their arms in the style favoured by string puppets the world over, attempted to deliver a serious message through the medium of an American talk show. Personally, I will take some convincing that American talk shows serve any purpose other than to make us thankful that we don't live in Alabama, but the kids seemed to lap it up. The use of a giant foam microphone as a prop persuaded even the most reticent pupils to open up in front of the whole school and the performers deserve praise for managing to keep 250 children sat quietly without once putting Pokemon on the overhead projector.

Whether all the children left as little angels vowing never to bully or pick on people again is another matter. As the show dragged on and the adults, if not the children (who were glued to the floor, in any case), got twitchier, it was possible to wonder whether anything other than the moment when an enormous ape ran amok on stage would be remembered. The ape interlude – real, incidentally, and not another product of a sleep-deprived mind – had the kids in stitches, but seemed to serve no real purpose as far as the story went, other than to give the chirpy young man a chance to dress up and chase his two young assistants. The ape's wrath also helped distract the children's minds from the main point. In the playground afterwards they talked about the ape, they made ape noises and they even pretended to be the ape and bullied their peers by mercilessly chasing after them; the one thing they didn't do was temper their behaviour and show extra consideration towards each other.

That's kids for you, too much energy by half. Of late, much of this energy has been put into the Christmas production, with children practising their parts as angels, wise men and stars (stars being the modern equivalent of sheep or apes – the acting part given to those who, even aged 5, patently can't act). The speed with which lines are learnt is incredible. At last count there were eight sets of lyrics to be learnt and yet even children who can't remember that $1+1=2$ can accurately remember 25 minutes of lyrical content. It would be great if their innate ability to learn stuff that is essentially useless could be tinkered for more positive gain, and to that end I have just finished Pythagoras the Musical, while Aristotle's Bottle – a mathematical word game – is on my to-do pile. Sadly, both are destined to join previous efforts Take Away in a Manger and The Singing Word Detective in what is already a vastly over-filled bin.

And there we have the crux of this chapter (don't worry, I'm just as surprised as you that this thing is going to have some sort of resolution) – children are just like adults, only in smaller bodies. That may be no great revelation, but what were you expecting? A word-perfect translation of the Dead Sea Scrolls? A simplified breakdown of Nostradamus? All those will have to wait. Today we have the simple observations that, like us, children prefer to do things that are fun, that children don't like to have learning forced down their throat, that children won't behave like robots and simply do as we want them to, and that children have a range of talents that the typical school day only begins to recognize. It is these factors that make teaching so rewarding. There is no quick-fix method that can teach all children all topics; strategies have to be adapted, plans changed and, most importantly, lessons have to be made relevant and fun.

I have read somewhere that children are always learning when they are enjoying themselves, I don't necessarily believe this to be true, but the reverse, that children won't learn if they are bored and de-motivated certainly is. When I have my own classroom I will try to make it a place of fun and learning, the sort of environment where children can learn fractions while dreaming of being an author, a footballer or even working in their own chocolate mousse factory. Best of all, all this will be in an ape-free zone, the monkeying around will be left to the kids themselves.

# 14 Sink or swim

On a postgraduate teacher-training course there is one phrase that keeps repeating itself: 'getting thrown in at the deep end'. There is no honeymoon period, few hours to whittle away drinking under-priced beer and even less time to be filled by random searches of the Internet library system (though I have had time to discover that they stock *Where's Spot* in Punjabi).

Within a week of the course starting you spend a first day in school, within a couple of weeks you go into school for a whole week and you get to spend three weeks in school taking on ever more responsibility and ever more lessons. Those on the undergrad course – apologies to any reading, any that aren't filling in to-do lists of how to fill their spare time that is – have it easy. That may sound like a snide swipe at the undergrads, and to some extent it is. They're younger than us postgrads, have worked up less debt, have better skin and are generally unsullied by years spent in labour. (Of course, when I say labour, I mean a collection of white-collar jobs – insurance sellers, estate agents, lawyers, bankers – the sorts of careers you really dream about as an optimistic 10-year-old.) However, I don't mean to criticize the undergrad course, merely to point out that their learning curve is far shallower. The maths, or math if you're American and find that adding an 's' makes the word unspellable, should be simple even for a typical Year 1 class. Undergrads take four years to complete qualification, postgrads take one year, ergo postgrads work four times as hard. Or something like that.

Getting back to the original point, though (and I really should given that after 300 words I have written little more than a bloated intro), if being on the postgrad course is akin to being thrown in at the deep end (incidentally, why is being thrown in at the deep end any worse than being thrown in at the shallow end – unless you can't swim, of course), then this past week has been akin to being thrown in while wearing concrete slippers. It has felt like being a woman in Medieval times under suspicion of being a witch, getting chucked in a river with the options being: a) swim, thus confirming you're a witch and leading to prompt execution OR b) drown, but get a posthumous pardon.

Sending me to my watery grave has been the fact that my class teacher, the person who should be there to observe my lessons, take the rest and, if necessary, restore order, has been off sick for the past week. Where before I only had to concentrate on teaching a bit of numeracy and literacy (maths and English to those of us older than about 14), now the class is mine all day, seemingly everyday. From the gentle calming before the morning register to the waving off into mum's arms, they are my responsibility. Admittedly, much of this responsibility is quite mundane – making sure they get their afternoon fruit, ensuring letters are sent out – but it's still nerve-racking in its own way.

Far more nerve-racking is having to restore order to a class who have realized that in their teacher's absence they have a perfect chance to play-up. While the mornings have generally been OK, the afternoons have been yet another task that's like painting the Forth Bridge. Every few seconds I have had to stop to tell someone or other to stop talking, then to tell someone to stop fiddling, then I've managed to start my sentence again just before the whole process repeats itself. What makes it worse is that I have started to feel my patience going and I'm starting to go back on plans of just staying cool, quiet and waiting for order to be restored naturally. It wouldn't happen – I'd be there until gone Christmas if I just waited for quiet. Instead, I have started to raise my voice, just a bit and always under control, but all the same it's a bad sign. Grouchiness has also set in, though this I feel is completely understandable. Just planning a few lessons a week is hard enough without the added pressure of taking the whole class for everything. Sleep has been replaced by worry, good humour has gone – tired resignation has taken its place.

But, as always, there is an upside. As everyone keeps assuring me, and I reluctantly agree, this is actually the best experience I could possibly have as it will obviously stand me in good stead in the long run. Perhaps, come Friday evening, I will start seeing it all in a more positive light. By then the teaching block will be over and I will have numerous beers, lie-ins, two weeks in college and then a holiday to look forward to. Roll on Friday.

# 15　Time to reflect

After three weeks hard graft in school, I returned to college with a sigh of relief on Monday. The time in school has been vastly rewarding, educational and enjoyable, but it has also been taxing, stressful and tiring. The three weeks, and especially the last week when my teacher's absence meant I was responsible for the whole class, felt like months; conversely the next month away from school will probably feel like days.

However, while it's nice to reacquaint myself with *Flog It!*, *Murder She Wrote* and *The Rockford Files*, the main benefit of our break from in-school training is that it gives us all the chance to reflect on our practice. While in school, I found it virtually impossible to analyse my own development. I felt like a man trying to stay on a roller-coaster ride without the aid of a seat belt. I certainly didn't have a hand free for any other task. At this stage, planning lessons seemed to take an eternity, choosing resources required endless trips to the stock room and any time outside of lessons was spent in assessing the class's learning and updating training folders. My three training folders are now each full to bursting with notes and observations that I know I will barely look at again. They sure will burn nicely once the course is over.

Now that we are back in the safe confines of the lecture hall, there is time to reflect. The lectures themselves seem to make far more sense now that there is some concrete experience to link them to, while the course reading list, an overwhelming series of charmlessly titled books, suddenly feels more important and relevant. It is back in college that you realize that your own experiences are by no means isolated, that everyone has some good lessons and some that are not so good and that no-one is finding the course to be a cakewalk. Actually, that's a lie. As on any course, there are those one or two people who admit to no problems and profess themselves to be superteachers in the making. Naturally these are the one or two people that everyone else seeks to avoid and secretly wishes all manner of misfortunes upon. For most of us, though, this week is extremely useful as we swap tips on classroom management, planning and all manner of titbits from where to park in the office car park to how much tea money we should have to pay each week. Personally, I pay £1 per week, which doesn't sound too bad for seven cups per day.

The other big topic of discussion, or at least the other big topic that's remotely linked to education, has concerned coursework. The course features the usual diet of essays and assessments, while for each core subject we have to complete a wide range of vastly different tasks. In a way it's a bit like the *Krypton Factor*, only without Gordon Burns or the sanitized army assault course. This week saw us handed back our first two essays, though to be honest I'd quite forgotten ever writing them as they were given in over a month ago. As ever, there was that fake panic as the essays were handed back, people who'd spent weeks researching every word pretending that they might fail, but of course no-one did. There was no drama, no squealing or sobbing, just rows of contented students reading and re-reading their comments pages or quietly chuckling as they glanced at their elongated bibliographies.

I might even read mine again at some point, though I'm not sure how much I would gain from them now. They were written at the start of the course, before I had done any real teaching or spent more than a few days in school. Just writing that makes it feel like ages ago. It shows how far we have all come on the course. While you're in school you don't really notice how much progress you're making, you're quite happy just to do the best you can and survive.

The time back in college is the exact opposite – you're actually learning less but there's far more time to reflect and think 'blimey, aren't I quite the bee's knees'. And so that's what I'll be doing for the rest of this week as I settle down with a vat of tea and look forward to two 'study days'. To anyone driving by my house it may look like I'm sat watching *Trisha* in my dressing gown while eating porridge and reading the Argos catalogue, but I'll actually be working hard, reflecting on the past three weeks in school. In about three weeks time I might have finished reflecting (or I'll have run out of porridge) and then I'll feel ready for a return to school and so the whole process will begin again, only with one slight change. I'll be that bit more confident and, hopefully, that bit more competent as a teacher and increasingly ready for the big challenge. Taking my first teaching job in September.

# 16 Students say the funniest things

One term down, two to go, and, with no other subject matter immediately apparent, it is a good time to reflect on what I have learnt so far as a trainee teacher.

Within the first few days of the course starting, I learnt that student fashion had changed little in the past ten years. Jeans are still baggy, hooded jumpers commonplace and T-shirts still have unamusing, supposedly amusing, slogans – 'Teachers do it standing up', 'My other T-shirt's a Ralph Lauren', 'Rehab is for quitters'. Ha!

I also noticed, and I put this down to some sort of post-Clinton worldwide depression, that students are far more serious and hardworking than they used to be. This point was rammed home mercilessly when, early on, I asked one of my peers if they fancied a drink and they came out for just that, one drink, before promptly returning to whatever they were doing in the library (checking how many languages *Spot the Dog* is published in, if they were anything like me).

Of course, the reinvention of the student population from a morass of Rizla-buying slackers to motivated self-starters can only be seen as a good thing (unless you run a student bar, that is). It is also entirely necessary as I have discovered that training to be a teacher is entirely unlike my other student experiences, namely six hours of lectures a week learning about modern European history and then countless hours learning the dark arts of journalism; drinking to get the creative juices flowing, drinking to mix with contacts and drinking to relieve the stress of a hard day's drinking. For a 150lb weakling I don't half have a beer gut to be proud of.

The course has been intense, probably more intense than any other period of my life. With training for most jobs the build-up is entirely theoretical and it's months, if not years, before you actually get to experience the job first-hand. With teaching it is the opposite, getting thrown into school so that on returning to college the lectures make more sense. To use an analogy entirely different to the one I used at this stage last week, it is like removing a newborn foal from his mother, throwing him into a tiger pen and then whisking it back out to give it a lecture on the danger of predators. It's kind of back-to-front, but it is also highly effective as already I feel fairly confident that I can stand in front of a class and keep them occupied without once having to whip out a bag of balloon animals. And that is probably the main thing I'll take from these past few months – belief. Changing from a job where all I had to do was write about sport all day and going on the occasional press trip was a risk. It is gratifying to know that I at least won't be a complete write-off in my new profession.

# 17 Cake eating days

After almost three weeks off (24,480 minutes to be precise, but who's counting) I returned to school this week for the next stage of my training, only to be faced with videos, informal chats and a mountain of cakes and baked-potato fillings. However, those of you already set to write in bemoaning the fall in educational standards and the lack of discipline in schools can relax, for this was no ordinary school day. This was one of those days that no-one outside the profession really understands, one of those days labelled by people I know as an 'extra bloody holiday for teachers' and one of those days where teachers get to ditch their old check jumpers for trendier stripy jumpers. This was an INSET Day (or Baker Day, or any other of the numerous terms handed down over the years . . . )

INSET Days had, until Tuesday, always been something of a mystery to me, both because I had never witnessed one and also because I previously had little desire to witness one. After attending just one, I might still not be the perfect person to explain what happens, but what the heck? I'm going to try. Essentially, they are training days. I'm pretty confident about that part, especially as INSET stands for In Service Training. Hopefully that explanation will suffice for most of you (after all, if you're working in an office and are just reading this to while away a bit of time why would you actually care what an INSET Day is?), but in case it doesn't here's a bit more information.

According to the School Zone website, INSET Days were introduced so that 'headteachers could bring all their staff together for training purposes. They should be an important tool for headteachers to help staff maintain and develop their professional skills and knowledge for whole-school development planning.' And so there you have it. INSET Days are a chance for the staff to get together, coincidentally often at the start of term or the day before a Bank

Holiday, and look at a specific area of development. In my school on Tuesday the area of improvement was ICT (essentially computers and other technology) – hence the video and, I suppose, hence also the informal chat. The session was certainly useful and everyone had the chance to play around with some resources and also have their ICT planning checked over. To be perfectly honest, I'm not sure how much I learnt. My ICT skills are fairly well advanced (a point that might be of interest to any would-be employers), but others seemed to have their *Blade Runner*-esque visions of RM Nimbuses dominating human slaves slightly assuaged. The INSET Day was also a nice easy reintroduction to working life after a Christmas break in which my most stressful task was getting up early enough to catch the ski bus. The following day was also great and I found it vastly reassuring to learn that, a few moans about getting up aside, I was really happy to return to teaching. In fact, I was so happy that I barely found myself thinking that it was about 500,000 minutes to my next ski trip. I reckon the time is going to fly by.

# 18 Teaching bad values

Tomorrow I will be teaching a lesson that my gut instinct tells me is plain wrong. The lesson is not in bad taste, it ties in with the curriculum and it even encourages healthy living; a selling point not to be sniffed at in an age where couch potatoes are getting too chubby to turn the television on. My concerns are that the lesson, and lessons of its ilk are, in the long run, entirely unnecessary and secondly, and most importantly, that it is sending out a message that I would not want my children (if I had any) to receive. The message is not that it is ok to steal, or that a dog is just for Christmas, or even that the tooth fairy does not exist; it is that it is alright for a youngster to grow up supporting Liverpool FC. After teaching this message I will be forced to have a good wash. In bleach.

Now you may ask why I don't just teach something else. The lesson aim is to use a variety of sources, including the Internet, to find out information about a famous person, so why don't I just plump for Jeremy Edwards, Ferne Cotton or any other run-of-the-mill Z list celeb? Well, I have chosen Michael Owen because the school has just been handed a shirt signed by the England striker – apparently such shirts are fairly common place now that Owen has 90 minutes to fill every Sunday night. One of the school's pupils (I have opted against using the term lucky) will win the shirt, so it seemed sensible to at least raise awareness among the class about a once pretty good footballer. Tomorrow, a class of 30 five and six year olds will pour over press cuttings, mostly from 1998, browse through a few magazines and look at a few carefully selected websites. Quite what the point of looking at the sites is, I'm not sure – it seems to be part of the current drive to teach every imaginable skill at the earliest possible age. No doubt it will soon be part of the curriculum to play tapes of Pythagoras' theorem to embryos.

My quibbles are not merely the moanings of an old technopho-bic dinosaur – I'm pretty keen on the Internet, having earnt a decent living on the back of it for five years. Being able to use computers confidently will be of great value in their later life. My doubts are whether they really need to learn the skills before they can even confidently recite the alphabet. Computers can be a great aid to learning for youngsters of any age, their buttons and the bright images on screen can make numeracy and literacy fun as long as things are kept simple. Overdo it and you risk burn out, a steep learning curve of learning followed by a long, disappointing plateau. Perhaps Michael Owen is the perfect subject matter, after all.

# 19 The standards

The standards, far more than any essay or subject portfolio, are the key to passing the whole course. Muck up an essay or two and you'll be coaxed through and will probably get the chance to re-write it. In fact, muck up an essay and, unless it's terrible, the marker will probably give you the requisite 40 per cent pass mark and that, unlike on a degree course where every mark counts, is all you need. Fail a standard, or to be more precise fail to achieve a standard, and you risk failing the course, at least until you have been back into school and filled in the blanks. That means missing out on graduation, missing out on the post-course relaxed beers of the successful and missing out on jobs. Schools can hardly take on someone who hasn't qualified, after all, so it will almost inevitably mean that you'll be looking for a job starting in January rather than September, a delay that eats into any savings (and you've done well if you reach the end of the course with any savings whatsoever). The standards are a catch-all system supposedly designed to ensure you can not only teach, but also run after-school clubs, organize out-of-school visits, brush your teeth, make a nice cup of tea and recite your own name. In Swahili.

Many of the standards are straightforward and can be ticked off with an arrogant flourish, others take a bit of work but require no shedding of sweat, while a few of them, the ones I colloquially nicknamed 'the bastards' are only achieved after either extreme effort or a bit of creative thinking towards the end of the course.

The standards come in a jaunty little folder known as the Professional Development Record (PDR). It is the sort of folder that you'll have to get used to in teaching as, even after training, teachers are required to keep records of their ongoing development and additional responsibilities, not to mention all the folders crammed full of notes and lesson plans pinched from the Internet.

If you fart as a teacher you probably have to make a note of it and put it in a folder somewhere. In that regard, the PDR is excellent preparation. If, like me, you start the course with a flair for disorganization you'll be pleased to see yourself turned into a fully functioning model of Teutonic efficiency. If you are one of those people who love keeping files, a mid-ranking civil servant perhaps, then you'll find the PDR as unexpected a pleasure as it would be to visit Blackpool and not be approached by 20 people offering improbable prizes for throwing tiny hoops over large pieces of wood.

As you might have guessed, I found the PDR a major annoyance. The problem wasn't hitting the standards, it was bothering to record the evidence and make sure it was neatly cross-referenced. With hindsight, I can only recommend that you use an efficient system – every time you get evidence of hitting a standard, tick it off there and then, file the evidence and cross-reference it in some way or other, the easiest being to put a symbol on the evidence (something like a red star) and then a matching symbol on the corresponding piece of the PDR. At the very least, make sure you keep the evidence in a big pile somewhere so that you can stick it and spruce it up the night before it's checked by a tutor or assessor.

A pain in the rear apart, what are these standards things? Well, the best way to explain is to give an example. Standard 3.3.14 (the numbering system having clearly been organized by a librarian) is about equal opportunities. As with all the standards, you can either be working towards the standard, have hit the standard or exceeded the standard.

The working towards section is irrelevant. If you haven't got a standard it's not much good saying 'ooh, but I'm working towards it'. At best it serves as an aide memoir to show the standards that you still need to focus on.

Under the toward section, the PDR states: 'You are beginning to recognize and respond to equal opportunities issues as you arise in the classroom, including by challenging stereotyped views, bullying or harassment, following relevant policies and procedures.' Firstly, I haven't got the faintest clue what it means by 'as you arise in the classroom'. Does it mean that the teacher only needs be aware of these important points as they are getting out their chair? I can almost imagine a conversation between trainee and teacher:

Trainee: 'Hi boss, you know that standard 3.3.14?'

Teacher: 'The making a cup of tea one?'

Trainee: 'No, equal opportunities.'

Teacher: 'Ahh, yes, you haven't got that one yet, have you. Brought any money with you?'

Trainee: 'Actually, that won't be necessary for once. Yesterday I dealt with some bullying, then I reported a pupil for racial discrimination and finally I read all the policies. They weren't very good, though, so I took it upon myself to re-write them quoting the latest European legislation.'

Teacher: 'Excellent. I can certainly tick off that you're working towards the standard. Oh, just a quick point, what was your posture at the time?'

Trainee: 'I was standing . . . Oh . . . Shit . . . '

Anyway. To hit the standard, the wording is pretty much the same, indeed it's exactly the same, just with the 'are beginning to' part deleted. You have to actually be doing it, rather than be beginning to do it. Whatever that means. Incidentally, to exceed the standard the only difference is that you respond sensitively. Given that if you were insensitive you wouldn't hit the standard in any case you could argue, on a purely pedantic point, that in hitting the standard you automatically exceed it. More important than my flights of fancy, or pinickity pickings, is getting down to actually hitting the target.

In the case of standard 3.3.14, you can hit it either in a lesson or by review at the end of the week. In assessing a lesson, something your class teacher should do at least once a week, they will have a sheet to fill in whereby they get to tick off standards as they see fit. As soon as they tick a standard off, that's it. Even if they later change their mind, you have the evidence there in black and white and that standard can be forgotten about.

And although this may sound like quite a tough standard, after-all how do you hit it unless you come across bullying in the class-room, it needn't be so specific. I found that, by just being respectful to all the pupils and being able to talk about the school's equal opportunities policy, the teacher was more than happy to tick it off. That will be the case with a vast majority of the standards, some in the first placement, with the mopping-up process in placement two. Many can be ticked off as soon as you have shown that you will make a basically sound teacher – for instance all the standards about planning suitable lessons, using objectives and resources, and monitoring and assessment.

For the monitoring and assessment objectives, standards which are more likely to be ticked off during the second placement, all that is required is that you devise a way of checking that learning objectives are being met. This might be through making notes as you mark, observing specific groups during lessons or planning tests at the end of each unit to find out what's stuck in their collective memory. It's also worth keeping sheets that keep an overview of the class' learning, acting as a simple checklist against key objectives, not because it is necessary to get standards ticked off, but because it's good practice and might make your life a little easier when you're teaching full time.

A whole host of standards at primary level concern themselves with the individual subjects. Hitting them in numeracy, literacy, science and ICT shouldn't present too big a problem as you'll be teaching these in the first placement. It is useful to discuss the lessons beforehand with the teacher, perhaps asking what evidence they'll want to see in order to tick the standard off, or what progress they want to see from previous lessons. They might be unwilling to tick standards off in your first couple of lessons, but by the end of the first placement you should be getting most of the standards relating to the core subjects ticked off. If the teacher keeps putting 'towards the standard' you need to have a quiet word. Tell them to pull their finger out and tick the 'satisfactory' column, or at least explain where you need to improve.

Not hitting these initial standards in the first placement is not a massive problem, though it does mean that you'll be playing catch-up in placement two. Instead of focusing on the dregs and then applying for jobs, your time in the first few weeks will be spent achieving standards that, but for fussy teacher, you would already have.

The fact that teachers have so much discretion is one of the major faults of the course. As the person who observes you everyday they are obviously best-placed to see your improvement, but the fact that some teachers will tick off standards like a greedy child opening doors on an advent calendar while others will be as reticent as a British pensioner on an Autobahn hardly makes it the fairest of examinations. To give an example, there were people on my course who had over 15 standards ticked off after one lesson and yet more by the end of their weekly review. Within a week they had completed half a set of standards designed to last for 20 weeks.

Other teachers, the realists, would only tick standards off sparingly, building up so that by the end of the first placement the pupil would only have a few left to hit. These teachers are the norm and actually the ones who are doing their job a lot better, afterall what's the point of being told that you are a brilliant teacher after just one lesson when you are patently still mediocre at best.

Unfortunately, the type of teacher you get is just down to the luck of the draw. What you shouldn't do is suffer in silence. If you have a teacher who, despite all your best efforts, won't tick standards have a quiet word with your tutor at university and hopefully they'll have a quiet word with someone at the school, asking exactly what you have to do in order to impress.

More annoying than the teachers are the students who brag about hitting endless standards. They are best ignored, gossiped about in the pub and barred from all course get-togethers. No one likes a show-off. Anyway, their bravado is just masking some deep unhappiness, or at least that's the thought I consoled myself with when, after describing a particularly hard day, I was told by a peer that they had been told that they were 'the best trainee I've seen in 20 years' by their class teacher.

However many standards you manage to hit in placement one, there will almost certainly be some left in the second placement. In primary, the main ones concern the foundation subjects, the Government's name for what they see as the less important topics. Over the course of ten weeks, with 80 per cent of your time spent teaching, there will be numerous opportunities to impress in each of the subjects. The process is the same as in the first placement, with the teacher observing at least one lesson a week, two or three if you have several standards to hit. The teacher only need focus on the standards that have yet to be hit, freeing them up to look for evidence that you've made the requisite progress.

In any subject, all the teacher should really be looking for is evidence that you have planned using relevant objectives from the curriculum, your lesson has been differentiated for the different abilities by adding in some extension tasks for gifted pupils and easier ones for weaker students, and that the timing and implementation of the lesson was adequate. To hit the standards, the lessons don't have to be award winners, they just have to show that you can plan and teach an adequate lesson, after all that's all that a fair few existing teachers can do.

There are other standards which present a bit more of a challenge. I found the standard that relates to planning out-of-school learning problematic as, when I was at school, none of the lessons in any way tied in to trips out. Fortunately, I helped out on a school trip to the opera and this was enough to persuade the class teacher to initial the standard (though I'm not totally sure she knew what she was signing as I hastily wafted it under her nose). Had this opportunity not arisen I would have had to use a theoretical base to pass the standard. It is possible, though not ideal, to pass standards from essays and coursework. If, for instance, in an essay about promoting positive learning you write about the importance of school trips, you have done enough to pass the standard.

This approach proved useful in passing the standard that requires you to show awareness of teaching pupils with English as an additional language (EAL). Teaching in Cheshire, probably the least racially diverse area of Britain, this was simply not something that could be passed in class and so, taking this into consideration, the course included a requirement to write an essay on teaching children with EAL. This is the best way to see essays, chances to get a few rogue standards ticked off by spending 500 words talking about inclusion, differentiation and gifted and talented pupils.

Hopefully a few creative lessons, lots of hard work in class and a few brown envelopes left on the teacher's desk will be enough to get all the standards ticked off. If not, don't panic. You haven't failed. Yet. Your final report from the teacher, a document you might be able to influence by mentioning beforehand that you have a few standards to hit, can include terms that are enough evidence to use against standards. If it says that you have shown respect for all pupils, then the standard that demands you treat all pupils with success has clearly been achieved.

An even more direct approach is to show the blank boxes in your PDR to the teacher and ask them to sign them off directly. It's probably worth formulating an argument before you do this, reminding the teacher how, several weeks ago, you did that thing that could loosely be construed as hitting the standard. If you do this on the last day, just after handing over a parting gift, it should work a treat. If all that fails and the teacher won't sign it off, the head won't, there is nothing in an essay that can be used and no vague terms in your report that might loosely apply then, as you already know, you're in a bit of bother.

You have two options at this stage. You could go into your final review with the rest of the standards ticked off and hope that no one notices. This may sound risky, but given the lack of attention anyone paid to my PDR I'd be fairly surprised if it failed. Even if they did notice, they would probably only ask you for some evidence that you tried to pass the standard and, as long as you had done something in your 20 weeks in school, they would most likely tick it off. The courses all want high pass rates and are unlikely to fail any student for the sake of one standard, it simply doesn't make financial sense.

The other option is to come clean and admit you didn't get it. At worst, this would mean going back to school for a few weeks and having to miss out on graduation (not necessarily a bad thing). A more likely outcome is that, after a brief discussion of how you tried to address the standard it would end up with the same result. Standard ticked off.

Standards, up until the last week of the course, were the most worrying part of my entire course. If I knew then what I know now, I would not have worried half as much. Teachers, especially in the second placement, will happily tick off reams of standards as long as you are half way decent and, if a mediocre teacher like me can achieve them all, then I'm sure you will walk it. And even if you don't walk it, the tutors are there to help. They are your friends, not enemies. Actually, that's an exaggeration. None of my tutors are on my Christmas card list, but I bear them no ill feeling (well, most of them, anyway).

After several months spent in school, my PDR meeting came down to a 20-minute chat, most of it about my former life as a sports reporter and the relative qualities of French and English wines – I added more to the first conversation than the second. The standards are designed to help you develop and to provide a framework that you need to be thinking about in order to become a good teacher. They are not there to catch you out and fail you – that is not what the Government wants, it isn't what the course wants and it certainly isn't what you want.

# 20 Relax, I'm doing fine

Up until a few minutes ago, I had a topic planned for this week's column. On reading one of my old columns I have decided to scrap it.

The column I read was from a couple of weeks ago. Ostensibly it rambled on about INSET days, however what got my attention was not what I had written, but what someone had told me as feedback. At first, the fact that it had received feedback was intriguing – to date I think I've had about five comments, one of those coming from a pedantic teacher who managed to spot a lone typo in 800 words and two coming cohorts from my journalism training school. This one was different. It didn't look to criticize and it didn't dig up old nicknames or, bizarrely, praise the worst left foot in football. It merely suggested that I sounded stressed and on the verge of quitting.

Now the first part of that observation might be fairly accurate. I am tired, I seem to have a mountainous workload, I still have shoulder pains from a bad skiing fall, the taps in my house are running brown because of work going on outside and I am currently writing a column at 1.40am, just five hours before I need to get up and start again.

What is entirely inaccurate, and somewhat galling seeing as it comes from a complete stranger, is the suggestion that I sound like quitting. And so I read the column again. And again. All the time looking for the passage that hinted at a hasty exit. And do you know what? It wasn't there.

What I read sounded like someone who was finding the course a challenge, but who was getting on with it while quietly making a few quid on the side through writing. And that's how it should read, because the course is a challenge; I knew that before I started and anyone contemplating starting a PGCE should know also that.

The feedback got me thinking, evaluating my time on the course so far and why I had made the switch to teaching in the first place. When you are in the middle of a placement, with some lessons going well, others less so, it can be easy to forget the bigger picture. So I took a step back and looked. I left my job for a new challenge. Am I getting it? Yes, absolutely. I also wanted a job that would be different every day and part of that deal is surely that in getting different days you get some good days, some exceptional days and some bad days. At present I get my fair share of bad days, but I also get plenty of the other, besides which the bad days are not really that bad. They also only come when I forget something, normally to set ground rules about behaviour, and so they are my own fault to a large degree. Again, though, that ties into another reason that I made the switch, to start a job in which I would always be on a learning curve. On the course and on the placement I often forget just how early on the curve I am. Thinking now, I realize that this is for the long haul. Potentially, I could still be teaching in almost 40 years time, so what does it really matter if the odd lesson goes slightly wrong now? Would the job really be that interesting if it could be mastered in a matter of weeks?

I would like to say thank you to the person who gave me the comment. It has made me think about the course and about what the future might hold. Prior to the course, I had been blasé. How hard can a postgrad course really be, I thought. A few weeks in school, followed by weeks ambling around college, a beer in one hand, *Spot Goes Home* waved dandily about in the other. It hasn't turned out to be like that at all and to be honest I'm glad. I wanted a challenge, I wanted something that would really test me and, to use, a terrible cliché I wanted to feel alive. Whether I feel alive now, at 2am, is a moot point, but I've succeeded in finding a challenge. Soon though, there will be a challenge that I am really not looking forward to. The challenge of job hunting and interviews. Now that will be a test . . .

# 21 No joking matter

With just two days left in my first placement, now would seem to be a fitting time to reflect on my time in school, and so I will. Just not yet.

First, to use the sort of journalistic hyperbole that I used to revel in when writing about Oldham v Colchester or some other equally life-changing event, I will comment on the shocking state of humour in schools.

Five-year-olds are getting less funny. It's scary, but true. To back this up, I will call on personal experience – some of it my own. When my dad was at school, if his stories are to be believed, jokes, like everything else, were better. If Steve Martin had turned up in his class asking for a five-minute open-mic slot he'd have been told to wait his turn behind fat Jimmy. By the time I hit school age, jokes may have lost some of their humour, but they had gained a certain international flavour thanks to continued Cold War rumblings.

What do you call a Russian with one hand? Andropov.
What do you call a Russian with a chest infection? Nastycoff.

Now though, if my school is anything to go by, jokes are merely a vehicle for the subconscious. Joke time in my class (not an official lesson) is so surreal that only a pretentious upper-class student, probably called Rupert, could ever hope to raise a giggle.

Take today's session. It should have been a nice five-minute filler before lunch, it turned into the most painful comedic experience since watching *Kings of Comedy*. Joke one started promisingly – 'Why did the cow cross the road?' The answer, which I can guarantee you haven't got, was 'to see the big fat pig on the other side'. Cue hysterics from the class.

Joke two started equally encouragingly. 'Why did the skeleton cross the road?' The answer, which is worth £10 to anyone who can guess it (ask the publishers for the money), was 'to get on his crashed motorbike and ride to the moon'. Perhaps if on some Hunter S. Thompson-inspired binge it might make sense.

The final joke (it was meant to last five minutes, but by this stage I was fast losing the will to live) came from arguably the brightest girl in the class. 'Why did the pig cross the road?' she started, unperturbed by the sight of my head disappearing into my hands. 'To cross over to the other side and be helpful and find God', was, of course, the answer. This final joke ticked every box. It didn't make any sense, it wasn't funny and, in my view, worst of all, it was horribly religious.

Who to blame for the shocking decline in jokes in school is the question and, thankfully, in this slip today, claim thousands in compensation tomorrow culture, a culprit is at hand, the National Literacy Strategy.

The Year 1 syllabus covers writing instructions, reciting fairy stories, writing in rhyme, performing plays, effective questioning and extending stories. All useful skills, but ones that may be of little relevance in later life. Joke-telling, a talent that can be utilized at parties, weddings and even, if used by an expert, funerals gets not a mention. All of which brings me round to somewhere near the vicinity of where I started. In my ten weeks in school I have learnt plenty, suffered the odd low day after a lesson has bombed and discovered first-hand the effects of extended sleep deprivation. Most of all, though, I have had fun. Fun listening to my class' questions, fun seeing their enthusiasm and fun watching them learn. In fact it's all been fun bar the one part that by definition really should have been.

# 22 Jack of all trades

After deciding one sunny morning that teaching was the career for me, sadly this sunny morning coming after I'd already trained to be a journalist, there remained one major decision. Primary or secondary.

Clearly, there were advantages to both. In secondary I could really put my history degree to good use, I'd teach a far wider group of pupils and age groups, and I'd get to choose from a far wider range of pies in the school canteen. In primary, though, I'd have pupils less likely to brazenly swear in my face, tower over me, or shout 'megs' as they cheekily knocked the ball through my bendy knees in football.

In the end, one factor made up my mind. My education is quite broad, I'm equally bad at everything a quipster might quip, and so it seemed far more tempting to teach a bit of everything rather than a lot of something.

So far on the course, that has not really been the case. The focus has been on the biggies, the core subjects, mathematics, English, science and ICT, and so that's pretty much all that I've taught. Actually, it is all I have taught, one tiny RE lesson aside.

That is all about to change. With the first placement behind me, it is now time to look forward to the final placement in which I'll be teaching, well, everything, in preparation for being a proper teacher in seven months. What a scary thought that is.

The lesson that stands out in the timetable is PE. I might never have mastered the forward roll, but put a ball in my hand or at my feet and I'm in heaven. I fully expect to be the one at the back, idly doing keep-ups while it's taught in college.

In the Friday afternoon slot comes art. Sadly my artistic talents are nil – a teacher once advised me not to waste money on stamps when I asked whether I should send a painting into The Gallery on

*HartBeat* – and so I'll be taking a modernist approach. Paper filled with scribbles, coloured dots on white canvas and dissected teddies in formaldehyde. It will be an excellent talking point at parents' evening.

That still leaves six other subjects to be mastered in about four weeks each. History, assuming I remember anything from my degree, should be a synch, while geography will be great to teach as there are numerous opportunities to get out and explore the local environment and also do projects on areas further afield.

All that leaves is RE, which I don't remember being on the syllabus when I's a lad, drama, music and something called DT on my timetable, which I assume is design technology. In a matter of weeks, I should be, if not an expert, at least sufficiently competent to teach them all. It won't be easy, but I'm still confident that I made the right choice in choosing primary. After all, who would want to teach the unification of Italy to a class of dissatisfied 14-year-olds?

# 23 The parent trap

When I was just a little boy, I asked my mother what will I be? Will I be handsome? Will I be rich? Here's what she said to me.

'Shut your mouth my son, the future's not mine to see. Now hurry up home you brat, I'm dying to have my tea.'

Actually she said nothing of the sort and I certainly didn't speak like an extra from *Annie* (I point this out so as to avoid going down the American route of finding myself sued for libel by my own mother). I use the ditty merely for illustrative purposes. My parents would never have dreamed of being so dismissive towards me. Others, though, do untold damage merely through their destructive, disdainful attitude.

It is a terrible thing seeing a child punctured by their parents' apathy, and already I have seen it too often. The example that really sticks in my mind came during my pre-course experience. A ten-year-old boy had spent the best part of two days producing an illustrated story that he took real pride in. His teacher told me that it was by far the best piece of work he had done, and praised him accordingly. That night, his fingers turned white through clutching the story so hard as he waited for his mother to turn up at school (late as usual) so that he could proudly display his work. Eventually she came, fag in one hand, packet in the other. Her son sprinted up to her, paper thrust out in front to reach her that bit quicker.

'Mum, mum, look what I've done at school,' he said.
'I ain't got time to look at your rubbish,' she said, pushed the paper away, stubbed out her cigarette, grabbed his hand and marched him back home for a night of television soaps in front of a television dinner.

That young boy came in the next day and was thoroughly demotivated, irritable and produced work well below his normal standard. Sadly, his mood had improved little by the time I left the school a week later.

His mother's disgraceful lack of interest might have been an extreme example, though I fear it was actually quite symptomatic of many parents, but the overriding problem is widespread. In another school I went to, only five children had anyone attend parents' evening on their behalf, and that's in a Year 6 class, the year in which they take SATs tests that will have a bearing on their future.

Elsewhere, I have seen home reading records with not a single entry during an entire year, homework books left empty or filled with work clearly done by an adult, and children who have PE kits with pumps two sizes too small. Anecdotally, I have heard of cases where children have needed intensive speech therapy just because their parents couldn't be bothered to talk to them as babies. 'They can't understand', being the lame excuse.

To be frank, it makes you wonder how much you can do for some children as a teacher. What is the point of creating a positive learning environment, making lessons interactive, trying to develop children's personal interests and always offering encouragement if all that work is going to be destroyed by a few hours of bad parenting every night. If intelligence is part nature and part nurture, then clearly teachers can only do so much. Studies might have suggested that 75 per cent of intelligence is inherited, but the general consensus is that the figure is nowhere near that high. Our environment plays a massive part in determining who we become and so parents, guardians and teachers must all strive to help their children reach their full potential. Most are brilliant at it, but some are shocking. The shocking ones need to remember that having children is a responsibility, not just a right.

# 24  Quick! It's alive, assess it

With the course focused on assessment at present, looking at the best ways to test five-year-old kids to within an inch of their lives, it's only right and proper that we are, the trainee teachers, also being assessed. Tests, portfolios and even the odd essay or two – being a primary school pupil isn't all fun these days and neither, as I have discovered, is being a student on study week.

When it comes to checking the progress of our pupils, we are rightly encouraged to think of more creative and engaging ways to bring assessment into lessons. The days of rigorous times-table testing have gone, in many schools at least, and in their place are self-assessment schemes and hordes of ongoing records destined for the back of files in the backs of dusty store cupboards.

One of the ideas I particularly like the sound of is an assessment box. Pupils comment on the lesson, what they have learnt and anything they had trouble with; it's all part of trying to foster a sense of responsibility for their own learning. Another idea is to let the class know that they will have to give assessment at a set stage. 'Johnny – I will be asking you what you have learnt about gravity in ten minutes time.' Apparently it works a treat in focusing the class on the task.

Unfortunately my school days consisted of testing, testing and more testing, often under the shadow of a big stick, and because of this my peers and are obviously not deemed ready for such subtle assessment methods. For us it's the humble essay, a chance to turn a bit of background reading and a few homespun theories into a 2,000 word summary of decades worth of academic research. Personally (as you will have noticed), I have never found 2,000 words anywhere near enough to start getting to the meat of a subject and so I'm delighted to report that the PGCE assignments I'm working on at present aren't 2,000 words, or even 3,000. They're 1,000.

The first task is to summarize the role of the teacher; to say what the teacher does and how they do it. To look at how they motivate the class, how they organize the class and how they cater for all interests. To study how they deal with pupil conflicts and expectations and interact with parents and other adults. All this has to be backed up with relevant reading and examples from both our own teaching and from lessons we have observed.

As I see it, it is a bit like trying to repaint the Sistine Chapel with a tester pot of Dulux. I will have something like 87 words for each broad topic, though by using a small font and squeezing the line spacing I might be able to up that to 88. But the limited word count aside, essays remain one of the most effective ways of testing adults' academic learning, after all tutors do not have the time to speak individually with all their pupils about each area of the curriculum.

Teachers do, though, and so have far more of a chance to really gauge how their pupils are working. The odd test is ok, necessary even to take a snapshot of the class's learning on a particular topic, but simply asking pupils about tasks and getting them to explain what they are doing can be far more revealing.

Assessment, like everything else, can be made, well if not exactly fun, a lot more bearable. Fortunately, I'll be able to go into more depth at a later date as we have a 2,000-word essay on assessment to complete, or in my case a 1,400-word essay once I've stuck this column in as an impromptu intro.

# 25 The course

In teaching it's in the classroom that you'll ultimately succeed or fail. If you have a natural ability to get the point across, make lessons engaging and to empathize with the class there's nothing you can't teach. And on the course, if you shine in the classroom, pass the standards with ease and get a brilliant final report you'll be well set for a successful career. As long as you pass the coursework, that is. It might seem ridiculous, it probably is ridiculous, but even if you're the world's best teacher – Robin Williams in *Dead Poets' Society* crossed with that nice primary school teacher in *Goodnight Mr Tom* – you won't be allowed to teach if you can't write a passable essay on differentiation in the classroom.

Sorry. That's a bit of sensationalism. The course would give you a chance to rewrite the offending essay, coax you through it and then stamp your head with 'pass' before kicking you out the door. Theoretically, though, in a neat reversal of the normal pattern of things, if you slack in college you won't make it into school.

And yet at times it is hard not to, if not slack, at least take it a bit easy during the weeks spent in college. The problem is that many of the lectures, and especially the tasks, feel like a bolt-on. In order to be deemed worthy as an academic qualification, a theoretical, lecture-hall and essay-based element is essential, even if at times it feels like an exercise in filling time that is already pretty well filled. This isn't to say that the time in college is not enjoyable. Nothing could be further from the truth.

At the start of the course, in a speech I imagine is replicated in every teacher-training institute up and down Britain, we were told two things. Actually, we were probably told loads more than two things, but only two things have stuck. We were told to expect the hardest year of our lives. Hard as it is to quantify such things – how do you weigh up the physical pain of falling on your face repeatedly

as a two-year-old, or suffering family bereavement against the stress
of a few late nights of planning – I'd say this was an exaggeration. It
made for a decent first line, though. Better than 'although this will
be quite a tough year, it won't be the hardest . . . ' It probably wasn't
the greatest sales pitch ever and, having told a roomful of people to
expect a hellish year, I was quite surprised to see that the roomful of
people didn't rapidly disperse to sign up on a media studies course.

The other thing predicted in the opening speech was that we
would make some amazing friends who we'd stay in contact with for
ever more (though being a man I took this to mean that we'd give
them a call every few years and perhaps send the occasional text
message). During this first meeting, and indeed the first few days, this
seemed like an unlikely boast as I sat through conversations about
Bolton town centre, the history of Crewe (admittedly a concise conversation), microbiology and the impact of privatization on the rail
system. Over time, and over beer, however, I came to see some of
these people as friends and I quickly realized that there was no one
on the course who could be classed as unbearable. Actually, there was
one person, but she'll hopefully be the subject of another book at
another time.

And, just when everyone was starting to build a small network of
friends and allies, the course did exactly what you would expect –
splitting the whole cohort into four groups with the main criteria
seemingly being to put people into groups with people who they had
yet to talk to. And so it all started again, a few more awkward conversations before the course kicked off proper.

Looking back, although the first couple of weeks were a challenge, it always is when you're grouped with new people and forced
to fast forward into working relationships, they were also hugely
rewarding. People who were strangers only a week earlier became
such good friends that it was hard imagining a time when you
hadn't known them – that is the sort of thing that can only happen
on a university course (or, I'm led to believe, in prison) where you
are living in other people's pockets and spending endless hours in
each other's company.

Even more than on a degree course, you will come to rely on
your peers. Every lecture you take will be with the same people,
everyone will write the same essays and face the same tasks and
everyone will arrive back in college on the same days to discuss the

last few weeks in school. If you have a partner who is the jealous kind, expect a few uneasy questions as you'll be seeing a lot less of them than of your 30 classmates.

Much of this time is pretty light-hearted. Even before starting the first big block in school it is patently obvious that the time in college is the easy time when, as much as it's ever possible, you can relax without too many worries. It almost has to be so for, enjoyable as the time in school is, it is horrendously stressful at times and if the course offered no let-up you'd probably never return. That is not to say that the time in lectures is one big laugh – try holding that view after three straight hours of English theory – as there is still an immense work-load to go through.

At the start of the course you'll hopefully have reasonable subject knowledge, but they'll be holes all over the place. These need to be plugged, a tough call in itself, and on top of this you've got to learn the theoretical base of how to be a good teacher, learn how to control and assess a class, learn the curriculum not just for one age group, but for all the age groups you might end up teaching and write a selection of essays and presentations. Looking back, it is a wonder that anyone manages to fit it all in during less than one year. Somehow, though, you will and the sense of relief and pride at the end is awe-inspiring.

The first few lessons are the easy part – the easy introduction to the easy part of the course. On the primary course, the focus is on the core subjects – literacy, numeracy, science and ICT, learning MS Word now being deemed more important than our past or learning about the planet on which we live.

And at first a teacher-training course is the course that just keeps giving. It's well worth taking a big bag as in the first week we were given a quantity of paper that was enough to deforest several small Amazonian countries and enough CD-ROMs to do something that would involve lots of CD-ROMs. Be used as an ornamental mirror in Wetherspoons, perhaps.

There is actually far too much information handed out initially and there are whole swathes of the stuff that I'm pretty sure no one on the course actually looked at. In literacy, for instance, I quickly filled up two box files – not with my own notes, but just from hand-outs – while another box contained CD-ROMs full of lesson clips and suggested resources. Eight CD-ROMs, each one crammed full of material, easily 30 hours of poor-quality videos to be watched on a computer monitor. The key is obviously to be selective as in amongst all the tonnes of paperwork and the long lectures are some nuggets that have to be learnt.

Learning the subjects you are going to be teaching is the first concern. By no means do you have to be an expert in all the subjects. For instance, numeracy has many teachers in a cold sweat and yet all you need is decent ability combined with good teaching techniques. It is similar to sport where the coaches are not necessarily as talented or naturally gifted as the people they are coaching, but they do have the benefit of knowing the correct methods and the ability to help their charges develop. It certainly makes the lectures a lot easier when you consider that you are only trying to achieve two main goals – to boost your subject knowledge (and this may not be necessary in your stronger subjects) and to learn the correct teaching techniques.

The importance of the second aim cannot be underestimated. Numeracy had never worried me. I was good at it throughout school, took an A-level and can still manage to mentally calculate my supermarket bill (a skill worthy of *You Bet*, if you ask me). However, I still relied on the techniques that I had learnt many years ago in primary school and it was only when I came to teach that I realized how big a problem this was. In a lesson on averages, the need arose to divide a list of numbers by six. My method, tried and tested many times, was to put 6 one side of a vertical line and the number to be divided, 228, on the other side. The method works by then trying to divide each of the numbers by six, working from the left to the right. I believe that it is a method that has not been used since about 1980. To me it was the easiest method in the world, to the class it might as well have been the formula to work out the meaning of life. A lesson which had been going perfectly instantly started to collapse and just because I had not bothered learning the division technique the class used. I had thought I could get away without learning it until we started the unit on multiplication and division, a massive mistake I realized as I struggled to get the lesson back on track.

Numeracy, or mathematics as I'm going to insist on calling it from now on, is the subject in which it is easiest to make such mistakes and it is also the subject that causes trainees the most loss of sleep. The reason for this is simple. In other subjects the teacher is far less likely to set a task that is patently unsuitable for the class. For instance, in literacy the lesson will often focus on either some form of writing or perhaps oral skills such as explaining, debating or storytelling. As long as the pupils have understood the task they can achieve, the differentiation will be in the fact that some pupils produce a much higher standard of work than others. Similarly, in art some children will naturally produce beautiful pictures, where others will be more akin to a plate of spaghetti Bolognese spilled on a sheet of paper. In history, weaker pupils will give very limited explanations as to why things happened, where talented historians will empathize with people from different cultures living hundreds of years ago.

In mathematics, if the sums are too hard they are simply too hard. There is no chance of succeeding at a lesser level, the end product will simply be either a page full of mistakes or a blank page. This will inevitably lead to short-term behaviour problems from unengaged pupils and longer-term problems with demotivation. No one likes to feel like a failure, after all. Oh, and if you're thinking of making it nice and easy, that won't work either. The gifted pupils will race through and present their work about two minutes into the lesson leaving you with the task of filling the other half hour or so. And don't even think about getting the Lego out.

Planning is key, but you can't even begin to plan before you have an idea of the sort of thing that the class should be learning and how the lesson should be broken down. That is where the lectures come in, as although your time in school is a learning ground, it would be all too painful if you went in with no ideas at all as to what you should be doing. With lessons broken up into handy little sections – mental starter taking ten minutes, main teaching taking 15, tasks taking about 25 minutes and then another ten minutes for the plenary – the lectures teach you how to go about planning for each section.

The key to getting anything out of the lectures is to make a note of the bits that will be really useful in class. Much of the theory on how children learn to read, or how their counting skills develop is fascinating in isolation and well worth a Ph.D. study, but it is my firm belief that it is this sort of knowledge that will be infused naturally from time spent in school. After a year spent with any class you will have a far better grasp of their learning patterns than you could possibly get from reading any number of educational texts or attending any number of lectures. Everyone has their own theory on such things in any case and so it is impossible to come to any sort of conclusion without acquiring first-hand knowledge in the classroom.

The trainee teacher hardly wants their head muddled with a load of psychobabble. Far more useful are the resources to be used in lessons. These can range from the really simple, for example, one of the best ideas on my course was for bingo in mathematics. A simple, fun game in which the options are endless, for Year 1 pupils it might be enough to simply mark numbers by questions such as 'higher than ten' or 'two more than seven'. Higher up the school, the same game can be used with questions such as 'mark off a multiple of five' or 'mark off the sum of 16 and 17'. Anything that feels like a game to the class is almost bound to work and I found that they love being practical, making and then playing with their own bingo cards, far more than they take to filling in pages of sums straight out of a textbook.

A similar little gem I picked up in literacy was to use a tape recorder in lessons. There are many pupils who have great ideas but find it difficult to put them down onto paper (EAL pupils being one obvious example). By occasionally giving the class the chance to record stories or scripts onto tape, these pupils were able to shine, taking real pride in hearing themselves on tape, and absolutely everyone enjoyed the lessons (not least me, having had the task of marking 32 books removed).

All of these little gems need to be stored somewhere and, more importantly, tried out in lessons. It is incredibly gratifying, not to mention time saving when a few simple ideas given out in lectures turn into excellent lessons, sparing the need to spend hours trawling through textbooks and the Internet trying to find suitable lesson plans. And you tend to already have an idea of what will work before you even get to the classroom as the nature of the course is to make everything very practical and hands-on. In mathematics this means playing little number games, in literacy writing short poems or describing a recent event. These sort of exercises didn't have anyone too worried, but some of the other subjects created a few beads of sweat – not least from me.

Art was always my worst subject at school, so lectures spent drawing, with the tutor seemingly glued to a spot just behind my shoulder for three hours, were stressful. Perhaps that is the point, though. The lectures are great at putting you in the shoes of the pupil, making you think about how they will feel during lessons. I'm not sure how intentional it was, but the points where you feel a bit out of your depth, in my case trying to draw a horse in full flight, or, most painfully of all, sing (even it was as part of a group and I wasn't actually singing), were very illuminating. If I as an adult in a roomful of friends felt nerves, it is safe to assume that there would be pupils petrified at the prospect of certain lessons. It certainly drums home the need to differentiate to make sure that everyone feels that they can get something out of the lesson.

Crucially, the lectures will also provide tips on subjects that you might have no idea how to teach. In design technology, our group created mini trucks, in art we made clay models and in music we created chants using basic percussion instruments. All were excellent fun; give me the choice between playing with clay or sitting at a desk and I'd chose clay every time. They also provided the planning for whole schemes of work. In art, a whole half term might be spent designing, drawing and then making clay models. Thanks to one lecture, what had seemed like a real problem area suddenly seemed much clearer and whereas planning even a single art lesson had seemed like a mammoth task, planning an entire unit now appeared possible.

Away from the individual subjects, there are also ongoing lectures in teaching studies, lectures aimed at putting the style with the substance. These lectures cover anything and everything you could ever want to know about actually teaching a class. Planning, assessment, controlling the class, working out how different pupils learn, differentiation, working with adults, working with parents, working with other teachers and planning your future as a teacher. If it sounds like a lot to get through that's because it is.

Fortunately it is not learnt in isolation. The first few lectures tend to cover fairly broad topics such as how to create a positive learning environment and how to teach an effective lesson. These sort of topics are perfect for the first few trips into school where there is time to observe and simply think about how the teacher goes about their craft. Later on, when time in school is spent teaching whole units with the class teacher often reduced to little more than a spectator, it is assumed that these early lessons have been observed and so the focus moves on to the finer points of teaching such as assessment or managing class behaviour.

Tied in to these are tasks that are replicated in some form or other on all teacher-training courses. In our particular course we were set four essays for teaching studies, or mini-essays at between one and two thousand words, to be more precise. The first of these focused on creating a positive learning environment. The aim of this was to provide a focus for the first few visits to school, with the essay broken down into subsections on the resources available and how they are used, the structure and pace of the lesson and how time was organized by the teacher. It is all stuff that you would naturally start to pick up, but the need to turn it into a passable essay certainly accelerates the whole process.

The second of these essays was equally broad, looking at the role of the teacher – sadly an essay saying that the teacher's role is to teach isn't quite good enough. A good essay in this instance would look at how teachers try to make lessons engaging for all pupils and also how they deal with wider issues such as bullying, motivation, the expectations of the pupils and their parents, and the pupils' own sensitivities. As these are reflective essays, a good pass can only be achieved by talking about practice you have observed and then relating this to how you will try to adapt your own teaching.

The third essay was far more specific, focusing on managing behaviour. Given that managing behaviour is probably the biggest challenge for trainee teachers as nothing can be learnt in a classroom resembling a monkey house, this essay offered a real chance to focus on a key issue. With behaviour management there are a number of theories, the main ones being the behaviourist approach which aims to control the class through a series of reprimands for bad behaviour, and a more Mind Friendly Learning style which accepts some levels of bad behaviour and tries to find practical ways of solving them (for example, giving a prolific fiddler a lump of Blu Tac to play with, rather than giving them a punishment for behaviour they are physically unable to control).

Essays of this ilk, though immensely annoying if you are anything like me and tend to leave them until the exact moment that a thousand other things start pressing on your time, are actually incredibly useful. They are also worth doing well, even if you do only need a 40 per cent pass mark. Writing the essay is a chance to really focus on a key topic and, from the wider reading, pick up a wealth of knowledge that you wouldn't otherwise have. There is a tonne of wider reading to be done on the course and inevitably some of it will only ever be glanced at by the most conscientious of students. It seems as if the essays are set with this in mind, to ensure that the bits of reading that are really important, the chapters on assessment, behaviour management and other key topics, are actually read and not just left indefinitely on a 'to-do' list.

The final essay in this series, and again a type of essay common to teacher-training courses, required real reflective thinking. The title was left blank, trainees had to choose an area of their own teaching they thought needed attention. From the list of a million possibilities, I chose planning, partly because planning is such a nightmare to get a grip on and also because various coursemates chose planning. Safety in numbers and all that.

Most of the individual subjects also place burdens on your time in school, with a series of directed tasks. These are invariably incredibly easy – one of the ICT tasks required nothing more than completing a quick tick box of resources in the classroom – and are generally more pointless than the teaching studies tasks.

Some of the requirements, such as writing about EAL pupils for literacy, are worthwhile additions, but others feel bolted-on, as if the tutors felt jealous of literacy's extra paperwork. Afterall, is it really necessary to know what size of boxes can be made from different length matchsticks, or to produce a PowerPoint presentation on health and safety in the classroom. (And what is it with PowerPoint nowadays? Boring notes put up on screen, talked through at great length and then handed out in mini-slide show format on A4. Thanks to PowerPoint, people the world over now get bored by the same facts three times over.)

The final assessed parts of the course are skills tests in literacy, maths and ICT. They actually get ticked off in the standards folder, but unlike all the others they cannot be passed in school. In each of the subjects, trainees must sit a test taking roughly 30 minutes, with the requirement only to reach a none-too-demanding pass mark. The very best thing about these tests is that, unlike a few years ago, you now get as many attempts as you like, all at no extra cost. In theory, you could take all three tests dozens of times, finally passing at the end of the course, and it would in no way stand against you as the number of attempts taken is not recorded. Such horrors should not be necessary, however. If you're confident in the subjects, you can take the tests straight away and get them out the way. If not book a test early and use it merely as a practice. You'll discover that they aren't all that bad after all. Literacy has a few spellings to correct, some punctuation to add in and a selection of reading comprehension questions. Mathematics is a mixture of mental arithmetic and slightly longer, calculator-based questions. And ICT focuses on those things that people do with computers every day – browse the Internet, write and save documents and send emails. Thousands of emails (although you'll only have to send two or three).

In total, if you wanted to count them all up (and that will probably be a mathematics requirement on some courses) there are probably about 30 separate tasks. It's an awful lot, and yet somehow they don't make the course any less enjoyable. Many of the tasks are ridiculously easy, while most of the rest are so obviously beneficial that they are almost enjoyable. Correction. Writing an essay is rarely enjoyable, but they are at least beneficial. There are a few tasks that appear entirely irrelevant to anything so when you do encounter one of these knock it out as quickly as possible and moan about it like everyone else does.

And mostly the course is great fun. It's throwing a ball around in PE lectures, playing music, writing bad poetry and watching embarrassed course mates pretending to be gazelles in drama. It should be taken seriously, but perhaps not too seriously.

# 26 Onwards and upwards

A new school: new teachers, new challenges and new children. It's all change on the PGCE course and I for one feel like the Littlest Hobo. It seems like only yesterday that I was in school one, teaching five-year-olds about complex two-dimensional shapes, while it was literally only yesterday that I was in college, giving an off-the-cuff presentation on creative learning; if memory serves. Today it was back to school only, like the tagline from a straight-to-video movie thriller, everything was different.

Instead of the sporadic movements of a Year 1 class, picture atoms bouncing around a jam jar, there was a certain calm. Pupils arrived quietly, politely asked who I was rather than staring at me as if I'd used acid for aftershave and then got on with quiet reading. They then sat quietly through literacy, responded to questions, worked hard and then quietly went to break. After that, they did some quiet mathematics, enjoyed a snowball fight in the playground, came back in quietly for quiet history before doing some more quiet reading and quietly going home. To sum up, it was bliss. Rather than feeling like a downsized Arnold Schwarzenegger in *Kindergarten Cop*, I felt becalmed. Here was a class that at least gave the impression of really wanting to learn.

However, it wasn't just the class' attitude that made the day so positive. If mistakes are for anything, then they are to learn from and having made an error in my last placement in being too circumspect when it came to asking the teacher for plans and assorted other paraphernalia, this time I simply bit the bullet and asked for the lot. Result – a heavy bag to lug home full of plans, class lists, ability groups, school policy documents and various other sheets that will probably remain unread.

Having had such a great day in school, it would seem the sensible thing to do to go back tomorrow and get to know the class a bit better. Sadly, course timetable planning and sensible seem to be words that will forever remain uneasy bedfellows. For the next two weeks I'll be back in college, making model cars out of cereal boxes, checking the rate of evaporation from assorted fabrics and throwing sponge balls to a partner stood about an inch away. All good fun, but not really as intensive a learning experience as testing yourself in front of a class full of kids.

In fact the big test is still 10 weeks away. On Monday 2 May I will start an eight week make-or-break block in school where I will teach pretty much everything. At the end of that I will either be given my framed teaching cardigan and slippers, or I will have my forehead branded with a big letter F and sent packing in the direction of Crewe Job Centre. The period leading up to the placement is the lull before the storm, but at least this time, after a great first day in school, my own waters are calm.

# 27 Keeping everything crossed

First for the good news. I've seen a job I really like the look of, I've read up about the school and some time next week a job application will be landing on their door mat. Now for the bad news. My application is likely to be one of at least 50.

Teaching jobs, it seems, are like gold dust. A few years ago, having qualified teacher status made you as popular as an attractive girl in a student bar on singles night. Now, though, there is a veritable glut of teachers. Apparently the situation should change again in about 10 years time, but I have my doubts as to whether my overdraft can last quite that long.

Clearly, the Government is to blame. For the past few years they have been ramming those damn teaching adverts down our throats. The message has always been 'do something amazing', 'who wants a nine to five job?' or 'fancy a nice uniform?' Actually, that might have been the recruitment drive for the police, but you get the idea. Incredibly, from a Government that has seemed unable to get any of its points across for the past couple of years, this message worked a treat. Thousands of people were persuaded to stop pen pushing in order to do a job that actually has some value. In fact, too many people, hence the huge number of applications per job at present and hence the scaling down of the advertising campaign. Those advertising men earned their thousands, completely ignored the message of their own campaign, and moved on to persuading people to sign up for duty in Iraq.

Had I known this a year ago would I still have applied for the course? – absolutely. There might be 50 applications per job (even more at present when there is only a trickle of jobs to fight over), but I am reliably informed that about half of these are generally rubbish. Without wishing to be rude, there are a lot of nutters out there and a lot of them are applying for jobs they are patently unsuited to. Sixteen-year-olds straight out of school apply for teaching posts. Bored midlife-crisis victims apply despite having no formal qualifications. And shop assistants write in because they think the job might be a bit more interesting than stacking shelves. However, that still leaves maybe 25 decent applications and so the law of averages would suggest that I'll have to fill out somewhere around that number of forms, have that number of interviews and go through the whole laborious process that many times to get a first job. Sod's law would suggest that the number will be higher still – perhaps somewhere in the low hundreds.

Sadly these sort of statistics are all too common. From personal experience, getting on a journalism course involved something like a 100 to 1 shot given the ratio of applications to places, getting a job was maybe 20 to one and then getting on the teacher-training course was a 60 to 1 shot. That last statistic was helpfully provided by the girl sat next to me just before my turn came for interview – it gives me no pleasure to inform you that I think she was one of the 60.

Looked at one way, the logical conclusion would be 'why bother?' The odds are so loaded against you for any course or job that it is barely worth applying. That, though, would be a terrible message for any teacher to pass on to their pupils. Far better is to look for the positives. All people are looking for is for someone who stands out, someone reliable with that bit of invention and confidence to try things. The ability to be themselves and to try their best. That's surely the whole point of teaching – not cramming kids full of knowledge, though obviously that plays a part, but drawing ability out from within. There's a big crowd out there, we're teaching them to stand out in their own special way.

# 28 The art of learning random facts

In education there is always a fad that is currently in vogue. I don't know that from personal experience, I've just been told it enough times by weary teachers for it to have shifted from the 'rumour – handle with care' part of my brain to the 'God's honest truth' part. Currently, teachers are spoilt. They have two fads – interactive whiteboards and Mind Friendly Learning. Both, to me, seem perfectly logical, not like fads at all, but then what do I know?

Interactive whiteboards are exactly that – part whiteboard, part remote-control computer. Naturally, some teachers hate them. Whereas once the only thing blighting their teaching life was the weekly task of operating the video, now they have a £3,000 gremlin in the room.

However, it's Mind Friendly Learning that I want to focus on. The name would suggest that it has come about as a reaction to Mind Unfriendly Learning, which would be a ridiculous concept if it wasn't so close to the truth.

If you wanted to devise a scenario in which someone definitely wouldn't learn it would go something like this. Sit learner down, lecture to them for an hour, set a couple of quick questions, end the lesson and then move on to a new area the following day. It's a method favoured by poor practitioners across the nation. The results of this method are entirely predictable. The information goes straight into the short-term memory, meaning that it can be called upon for those end-of-lesson questions. Seeing this, the teacher assumes they have done their job in explaining the new concept and move on and in so doing fail to make the necessary reinforcement that transfers information into the long-term memory. Several weeks later, the teacher cries out in despair, 'we did this the other week' being the refrain of choice, when a quick test shows that the class have actually learnt very little.

Mind Friendly Learning is all about making it easier for the brain to hang on to those pieces of information that we deem so important – Pythagoras' theorem, the capital of the Democratic Republic of Congo, the melting point of mercury – those sort of things. To sum up several thousand research papers and years of academic study in a few words, it's about helping the brain to make connections that establish learning as part of a big picture.

According to the Mind Friendly workshop I went to today, it's about understanding how the brain works (at least on a basic level, we're not brain surgeons after all). The brain, and I'm putting this as fact even though I only heard it a few hours ago from a total stranger (the paperboy, since you ask), doesn't actually want to learn every piece of new information. If it wasn't selective we'd simply overload. I've decided to call it the Sherlock Holmes theory, based on the fact that the great detective didn't know simple facts like the names of the planets, claiming that clogging the brain up with useless information only served to slow down the more vital functions. Admittedly, it's a theory pinched from a fictional, drug-addicted private investigator, but then he wasn't wrong about much else.

To counteract our brain's natural reticence to take on extra work, knowledge has to be reinforced, revisited the following day, the following week and the following month. It also has to be given some relevance and applied in a real-life setting. It's like learning foreign languages – probably everyone reading this learnt a language at school and yet only a handful will be fluent, and that's despite up to five years study. The reason is simple, without making the link of applying the skill in a real-life setting, for example speaking French in France, it won't ever become an automated skill.

I could go on, but there's really no point. Mind friendly learning (MFL) preaches that we only actually memorize things from the start and end of a lesson so, assuming that also applies to columns, the middle of this is already a dim and distant memory (as it is for me, too). I could have written any old rubbish, and indeed I did, but then what's the point of wasting great prose on the deliberately dysfunctional human brain? That's right – none what so ever. It's far better that I give you a piece of fascinating information to finish with as that's the bit you'll actually remember.

And so here goes, the capital of the Democratic Republic of Congo is Brazzaville. Got it? Good. I'll be testing next week.

# 29  The school of hard knocks

A couple of weeks ago, I wrote that I was about to apply for a position at a local school and so now is the time to let you know how I got on. Some people – my parents, my brother, my little sis' and possibly my wife – have probably already guessed how it went from the lack of gloating and extravagant splashing out on white goods in anticipation of a pittance of a salary. For those of you still in suspense, those of you who can't work out who dun it in *Columbo* until the denouement, I'll spill the beans. I didn't get it.

I'm not bitter, though. I don't mind because it probably went to a better candidate, there is probably a better job in a better school out there and, most pertinently of all, I couldn't really expect to get it after changing my mind by not sending in an application after all.

The reason, for once, was not abject laziness, I chose not to apply simply because of a 'bad vibe'. Prior to my about turn, an unfortunate character trait I blame on my suppressed Italian genes, it seemed like the perfect job. Perfect kids, in a perfect school. I had even started to picture myself turning up on my first day as the cool new teacher in a shiny new sports car – a vision so implausibly inaccurate on all levels as to be beyond any sort of analysis.

So to answer the inevitable question of what changed, the answer is one phone call. This was no ordinary call, ordinary for me being 'alright, yeah, yeah, what time? ok, see you later, bye', it was a call of pure deflation. The type of call I perfected about eight years ago, ringing an unappreciative girl after a boozy trip round Swansea's high spots.

The woman who answered was a leach, sucking my life down the receiver with her snotty, snooty attitude. The school had a date for applicants to come and view the school, however due to other commitments I made what I thought was a reasonable request, asking if I could come another time, before or after school if it helped. This, she said, was out of the question, her exact words being 'We don't have time to accommodate individual requests when we are expecting so many high-class applicants.'

Feeling pretty crushed, I considered hanging up there and then, but desisted so that she could insult me anew. 'Have you been teaching long?' she spitted. I explained that no, I hadn't, I was a few months away from getting my teaching stripes. This shouldn't have been a particular problem, the blurb saying that newly qualified (or qualifying) teachers were welcome to apply, however I now realize that what it should have said is that they were welcome to apply so long as they harboured no hopes of their application actually being considered. Miss Snot made that much abundantly clear, joyfully informing me that 'NQTs can apply, but the school is hoping to employ a teacher of an overall higher calibre.' Dumb as a dog, I still asked for an application form – cool teacher in sports car would have told her where to shove it – and that application form is now covered in Polyfilla, plugging an alarming hole in the garage.

Since then, I haven't seen anything else to apply for and so live in hope that April's showers also bring the torrent of jobs that I've heard about.

But the point of this column was not to bemoan my own employment prospects. There is a right way to treat people and the school I rang failed in their duty to show common courtesy and respect. I'm intelligent enough to realize that I might not have been right for the job and I hope, if only for the pupils' sakes, that they do indeed get a high-quality teacher in. What concerns me, though, is the school's attitude. They were wholly inflexible, took no interest in me as an individual and could have damaged my self-esteem. To me that would seem like a pretty damning indictment of any company, but of a school it's shocking.

# 30 Scared witless

One of the best things about being a teacher, or so I always assumed, was the holidays. Right now, unbelievable though it might seem, I am seriously beginning to doubt just how much of a good thing they really are. For the past 10 days, our course having broken up a week before the schools, I have been a man of leisure and frankly it sucks.

Prior to the break I had planned great things. Not great things in terms of endeavour you realize, but great things in terms of getting a bit of work done, applying for a few jobs and, most importantly, kicking back, having a few beers and chilling.

Of those, let's look at the jobs first. Apart from a trickle in the last few days, there have been precious few even worth considering and so the bulk of my applications will now inevitably be made at just the time when I'm back in school and have the least amount of time available. If that sounds pessimistic it's because it is, and I am.

As for the getting work out of the way, I'm afraid that has slipped too. I blame my disease – laziness. My aim was that, with my block placement starting in May, I'd get as much planning out of the way as possible. Needless to say, actually knuckling down to the work with more than a month to go is easier said than done and I already know, with grim certainty, that my planning will come down to a few late-night sessions in the fortnight preceding the placement.

However, please don't think that I have been entirely inactive during my break. Being married means that I have been lumbered with all sorts of tasks that I would never have even considered prior to my nuptials: painting, varnishing skirting board, fitting carpet, fixing a loose tile, sanding and then repainting window frames. If this is what my holidays as a teacher will entail then I say work the kids to the bone. Holidays, schmolidays.

Oh, and did I mention kicking back and having a few beers. Well, it seems that not everyone has two weeks off at Easter and so my friends were singularly reluctant to go on boozy midweek sessions or agree to budget flights out of Blighty at a moment's notice.

So, taking tonight as a typical example, rather than doing planning, or watching England down the pub, I have glued gripper rod to a concrete floor before settling down to a night of telly.

Currently it's *Ring* – the Japanese original – and I'm terrified. I'm in a dark house at 1.30am watching the denouement of one of the scariest films ever made, whereas if I had work tomorrow I'd be safely tucked up.

To be totally honest, I hadn't even intended writing this column just now, I started merely to take my concentration away from the film for a bit. But now, with 15 terrifying minutes to go, I've come to the end of this column. I'm tired, my nerves are shot and all I've got to look forward to tomorrow is trying to fit 44 square metres of carpet into a room that measures three metres by two metres. To top it all off, Sadako's just started crawling out of the well . . .

Now I feel like I need a proper holiday.

# 31 No room for manoeuvre

Far be it from me to criticize the National Curriculum (NC), after all what could be better than for a centrally appointed body to decide what every child in Britain will learn, but sometimes the intransigence of the document is simply galling.

Clearly worried that not everyone entering teaching was a genius capable of confidently planning and delivering a balanced syllabus, the NC came about to give teachers everywhere an identikit framework to work from. As a result, you could pick an age group, then visit classes up and down the country and chances are the pupils would be learning exactly the same things at exactly the same time of day. It is, of course, a marvellous idea – especially if you believe yourself to be an Oceanian fighting an interminable war against Eurasia.

The genius of the NC is that it stops cocky young teachers from getting carried away with themselves. To use a personal example – personal examples being so much easier than ones involving other people due to the lack of research required – I was delighted to discover this week that my degree will be entirely useless when I start teaching. A degree in history, you might assume, would be advantageous when it came to teaching history. With assumption, being the mother of all muck-ups, you would be wrong.

History, at least as far as the NC's authors were concerned, is a very narrow subject and as such there are only a few topics worth learning. As a Key Stage 2 teacher, you teach one world study on an ancient civilization, a local study, modules on Britain ranging from Roman times until modern day and a European study. The European study should be my chance to impart some quality learning as I spent five years studying the Weimar Republic, Nazism, the rise of Fascism, the unification of Germany and Italy, Communism in Russia, the Irish problem and numerous other modules. I believe each of these areas to be truly fascinating and, most importantly, still of great relevance to our lives today.

Marvellously, instead of teaching any of these, I will have no option but to enthuse my pupils about Ancient Greece. Part of the remit will be to study how the Ancient Greek way of life has influenced our way of life today, though I have a sneaking suspicion that it has slightly less of an influence than, say, the Second World War.

Despite the narrow remit, I fully intend giving my pupils a broader base to work from. It won't be too hard to include modern European history in with some of the British modules – for example, looking at Britain's responses to the troubled 1930s in Europe. And, in the unlikely event that anyone in any way linked to the NC reads this column, may I make a couple of small recommendations. Firstly, if you want to attract high-calibre recruits into teaching it might be an idea to let them use some of their skills and knowledge once they are in the classroom. And secondly, if you want children to learn about Ancient Greece call the module 'Ancient Greece'. Don't bloody call it a European history study because, as far as I'm concerned, it isn't.

# 32  Planning

As I believe I might have mentioned elsewhere in this book, in about eight places at a rough guess, planning is a nightmare. It is a particular nightmare for trainees, but it is a nightmare for all teachers. It is the single thing that turns teaching from a normal job into one that will expand to fill every waking minute and, for trainees, that can be a lot of minutes. And yet, despite planning being so hard and so time-consuming, many trainee teachers actually try to make it harder for themselves. I know this because I was one of those teachers.

It comes from the need to be more than just an identikit teacher. Anyone, or almost anyone, could pass a degree and, given enough luck and persistence find themselves on a teacher-training course. They could then, through doing just about enough, scrape through the course, land a job somewhere and go through the motions for 40 years teaching uninspiring, non time-consuming lessons. At the end, they'd get a nice pension, a few cards from the kids and no one would really miss them all that much.

That would be enough for some people. Fortunately, it is nowhere near enough for most. Pretty much everyone who starts a teacher-training course wants to be a really good teacher, for themselves and for the pupils in their class – all of whom deserve a top-class education. This desire to be, if not the best, at least the best you can be, impinges on the whole course. It ensures you do wider reading, put effort into essays and put across a professional image in school, but most of all it ensures that you prepare well for lessons. It is in teaching lessons that your effort, or otherwise, will be most apparent as the class will either be engaged and learning or they will be disinterested and a rabble.

And so I found that, especially in the first placement, I approached planning from a position of wanting to teach great lessons coupled with a fear that whatever I taught had a real possibility of bombing.

I also made the common mistake of refusing to take the help that was available. At the start of the course I took not being an identikit teacher to mean that I had to plan every lesson from scratch, forsaking all textbooks crammed full of lessons, Internet sites and even course handouts. It is a common mistake that trainees make in thinking that it is almost cheating to 'borrow' lessons from elsewhere. There is a sense that you are not really teaching at all, merely delivering a script if you take a lesson wholesale from elsewhere and, to an extent it is an accurate belief. However, the opposite, the idea of re-inventing the wheel is even more damaging.

At least in taking the seemingly easy option of taking prepared lessons from elsewhere you should end up teaching a passable lesson. If, instead of this, you try to plan all lessons from scratch, even when you don't have the skills to do so, you are setting yourself up for a series of disasters. Both poles have their benefits and their disadvantages. In taking too many pre-planned lessons your role is reduced to that of an actor. Admittedly, the teacher is a social actor, morphing their personality to become more confident and authoritarian in front of the class, however by not adding in any of their own teaching input they are no better than an actor reading through their lines. Worse still, although the lessons may pass without incident, it is an approach from which little can be learnt. It is the sort of thing they would probably do on *Faking It*, making it easier to adapt to a new profession in a matter of weeks. It is *not* the sort of approach that the trainee should take as they will gain no knowledge of how to plan lessons other than to see planning as copying pinched lessons into their own scrawl. And, with the course designed to be the training ground before entering the profession proper, the question has to be asked as to whether key skills missed out on during the course can be acquired at a later date. I have my doubts as, once the pressure of having your own class full time hits home, it would be hard to move away from ingrained, lazy practices. But if this approach is unsatisfactory because of its lack of invention, the idea that, as a trainee, you can ignore all advice with regard to planning is, while perhaps somewhat noble, both unrealistic and potentially damaging to the pupils who could be exposed to a series of unsuitable, incoherent lessons.

Clearly, the problem with this approach is where to even start. Looking at a blank page, knowing that you have a maths lesson to plan on division, but without any experience of planning such a lesson can lead to a long night – most of it spent staring at that same sheet of blank paper. I found that this approach also led to more false starts than the typical Olympic 100 metres final. Out of desperation, hours after sitting down to plan the lesson, you put something down only to be filled with self-doubt and cross it out again.

And so the key is obviously to find a balance. Use some of the help that is available, and also strive to bring your own stamp and ideas to the lessons and the classroom and, above all, don't become a martyr to trying to teach the perfect lesson.

Like all things on the course, planning gets much easier with practice. On the first placement you have a relatively light teaching schedule and yet I found that I spent more time planning for this placement than for the longer, supposedly more intense, second placement.

At first, in the day visits to the first school, you are unlikely to teach more than the occasional, isolated lesson. This sounds like a fairly straightforward task and yet it is actually quite a challenge. The lesson has to fit in with both the preceding and following lessons from the teacher and also stand alone as a valuable lesson in its own right. This task is even harder during the early visits as you will be planning a lesson to be taught in a week's time and, depending on how other lessons have gone in the interim, it might no longer fit neatly into the teacher's longer-term plans. For these early lessons, with the benefit of hindsight (which is the main benefit that this book offers), I would aim to plan a fairly safe lesson. Rather than try to plan a brilliant, but risky lesson full of amazing, off-the-wall tasks, I'd go for something that should go off without incident and, in the process, act as an invaluable confidence booster.

Sounds easy. So how do you go about planning such a lesson? The first step is to turn to the main source of knowledge in the classroom. Not a textbook (well, hopefully not, though in some classrooms you have to wonder), but the class teacher. At this stage you are trying to teach a lesson to tie in with their plans, so ask what sort of things you should cover. Your teacher, unless you've got a particularly bad one, should also help you choose the learning objectives.

Learning objectives, as you will soon discover on the course, are the key to teaching nowadays. At times, especially early on in the course, it seems as if lessons are only valid if they hit a whole host of them. Choosing learning objectives at this stage can be done fairly easily. Broad objectives are located in the National Curriculum, though these are only broken down by Key Stage. For more detailed objectives in literacy and numeracy, the subjects you will teach more than any other in placement one, you'll need to turn to the National Literacy and National Numeracy Strategies (NLS and NNS). These documents are idiot proof guides to what to teach. For experienced teachers they must be incredibly insulting – the idea that excellent teachers who have been safely going about their business for years get placed in a centralized straitjacket is somewhat repulsive, but it at least makes teaching easier for trainees.

In numeracy, the strategy lists everything that should be taught for each specific year group, with key points marked in bold. For example, under the heading Estimating, Year 1 pupils should be able to make a sensible estimate of up to 30 objects. Following the list of all the objectives for the year, it then gives an outline plan of what should be taught when, for instance in the autumn term Counting and Properties of Numbers should be the first thing taught, followed by Place Value and then Addition and Subtraction. Just to make the strategy a bit more interesting, this pattern is repeated in every primary year and so visit any primary school in the first week of the new term and chances are that every single class will be learning about properties of numbers in their numeracy lessons.

Literacy is even more prohibitive in its attention to detail. The entire primary experience is broken down into the 18 terms ranging from the autumn of Year 1 to the summer of Year 6. For every term, the strategy gives the range of what should be taught – for instance stories and poems with familiar settings, and instructions in Year 2, term one.

With this level of detail, you should be able to decide on objectives pretty quickly. Afterall, there really isn't all that much choice. Choosing objectives, though, is only the first bit of the battle. The next task is to turn these into some teaching and activities. For the first lesson or two it is definitely worth asking the teacher for some advice on what sort of activities work and, more usefully still, where they get their ideas from. It is well worth trying out a few recommended ideas at this stage rather than worrying about creating your own from scratch as this will free you up to focus on what, at this stage, is a more important goal of simply building confidence in front of the class. Only by trying these suggested ideas will you start getting an idea of what sorts of lessons you think will work for you. It is a bit of a moot point, but it may also be seen as arrogant and insulting by the class teacher if you don't turn to them for any advice, instead trying to do it all on your own.

In my initial lessons I tried to do too much on my own, coming up with activities that were slightly too difficult for the Year 1 class in numeracy and a bit lengthy in literacy. It was only when I had picked the teacher's brains – for instance simplifying numeracy by playing simple counting-style games and setting more specific literacy targets such as getting six lines written – that I saw real improvement in my teaching and could use this basis to start developing improved lessons of my own.

My main problem, however, was with timing. In cricket my timing was always off, my timing with jokes is off and my timing for work was notoriously bad. Unsurprisingly, it turned out to be just as bad in the classroom. Timing, at least for trainee teachers, is incredibly important. Lessons are supposed to be divided into neat little chunks of the mental starter, main teaching, activities and plenary. The starter and plenary should take about 10 minutes each, leaving 40 minutes for the bulk of the lesson. The trainee strays from this protocol at their own peril, especially when it comes to getting standards ticked off. Initially, this timing is almost impossible to quantify. In one numeracy lesson I'd planned an activity that saw the pupils each have a set of Post-It notes with their initials on to be stuck on any rectangular or conical shapes. The winner, the person who had put the most stickers onto suitable shapes, would get a couple of housepoints. In my plans, this activity was scheduled to last 20 minutes. In reality it occupied them for five at most.

Conversely, another lesson's aim was to end up with a drama performance of Cinderella. I had figured that 20 minutes would easily be enough, whereas in reality it took 15 minutes for the class to agree on roles and by the end of the lesson little more than one line had been mastered. From this I learnt that only practice makes perfect with regard to timing and also that letting pupils decide on their own roles in plays is a decidedly bad move – unless your play is entitled 'The 31 Cinderellas and their ugly sister'.

As a general rule, trainees find that they plan too much for lessons and are faced with the problem of having to miss chunks of their lesson out. While not ideal, this is at least better than finishing 20 minutes early with nothing prepared to fill time. Even five minutes with nothing planned and without the confidence to go off on a tangent can seem like a lifetime. Children, for all their great qualities, have notoriously short attention spans (their age minus two minutes being one theory of calculation) and so it's well worth going into any lesson with a few back-up ideas, even it's just word-searches, or jokes that will fill in a few minutes.

After a few lessons, such tactics won't be necessary as planning an hour-long lesson is actually not that hard at all. Just remember, hundreds of thousands of teachers all over the world plan and teach endless millions of lessons every year. If it was as hard as it might seem at first would they not just give up and look for an easier life?

The initial problem is seeing the four stages of the lesson as adding extra problems. If it is hard to manage the time of one lesson, then surely dividing it into four parts only heightens the challenge as each one could miss its target time by some distance, making the overall length of the lesson fluctuate madly? Actually, the opposite is true. Planning an hour's worth of material is extremely hard work. It is almost impossible to mentally quantify just how long everything will take, whereas planning 10 minutes or so is a fairly straightforward challenge. And so in planning lessons it is worth, at least initially, not worrying about making too coherent a lesson, instead focus on producing four good sections.

All lessons, at least all lessons taught by trainees, should start with some form of mental starter. This acts as a warm-up to the rest of the lesson and should also reinforce some previous learning. In numeracy, it is often as simple as games that recount tables, counting skills, or answering a few simple questions, perhaps similar to those set the day before, on whiteboards. This session is relatively light-hearted so work should be done in the head or on white-boards, rather than straight into exercise books.

In literacy, especially higher up the school, the starter is often shared reading, with the teacher leading the way as the pupils read and follow a text. It is hard to use this as a starter too often as, in my opinion, shared reading is one of the best experiences in school. All the pupils improve their reading skills, both mechanically in terms of just reading the words and also more advanced skills such as intonation and reading meaning into the words. It builds a real sense of class community with everyone joining in the same activity – even the weakest pupils get lots out of it as their reading will improve as they get challenged by more difficult texts. And, most wonderfully of all, it is the teacher's chance to impose some brilliant literature onto the class. In today's autocratic world of prescribed curriculums it is a rare chance for the teacher to teach what they want and to pass on some of the stories and texts that have influenced and enchanted their lives.

When you fancy a break from shared reading, the other main starter sessions for literacy involve word-level work. The objectives for these are stored in the NLS, with each term including about 20 word-level objectives. In Year 1, these include investigating simple rhyming endings and using them to spell words – for instance, writing the word bat and then asking the class to think of other words with the same ending. In Year 5, an objective might be to investigate words with ir- and il- prefixes, find examples such as irregular and illegal and discuss what sorts of words these are.

In other subjects, the formula is not quite as prescribed, but it still pays to include some sort of introduction. With most subjects only taught once a week it is well-worth introducing the topic at the start of a new unit and then, in each subsequent lesson, using the first few minutes to go back over the previous week and talk through any misconceptions you have noticed in marking work. After the starter comes the main teaching input – the part where the teacher earns their money. Having already chosen your learning objectives, you should have at least a vague idea of the sort of things you want to do. For instance, if your objectives are to look at pen and paper methods of solving division you know that you are going to be putting some sums on the board and talking through methods to solve them.

In literacy, if the objectives are to write simple instructions your teaching is likely to include a look at appliances or lists that include instructions, followed by a session of brainstorming where the class think of ideas for instructions for some task or other.

The key to this session is having decided on one or two key objectives and then thinking of what you actually want the class to learn. On the course the need to think of objectives in child-friendly language is continually pushed, for example 'To write a newspaper-style report of a sports match' (perhaps after watching a brief video), rather than the somewhat pompous 'To develop a journalistic style with balanced and ethical reporting'. This simplification also makes it far easier to start planning objectives.

The most crucial piece of advice I would give about the teaching input is to avoid trying to teach too much. It is tempting to aim to make great advances in each lesson, but people actually learn by adding little chunks onto what they already know. Take a fairly simple objective that builds on some prior knowledge, work through it with some good examples, give the class a chance to have a go so that you can look at any problems and then set them to task. The danger of trying to impart too much knowledge in a single lesson is that the message gets mixed and none of it actually goes in. The main teaching input and the tasks are always closely linked. It is your chance to check how the class have coped with the new idea and their chance to have a go at what they've just seen be explained. The activities, rather than being separate from the teaching, are merely an extension to it. In science, where the teaching might look at adding a bulb to a circuit and how to do it, the activity might be to experiment with different circuits, seeing what difference adding batteries and extra bulbs makes.

I deliberately haven't said too much about the activities because the best way to learn is to plough through some of the endless examples that are available in textbooks and, increasingly, online. For any topic, it is now easy to find dozens of lessons and although you may not want to follow their format exactly they do make excellent starting points.

The best starting point is the Qualifications and Curriculum Authority (QCA) Schemes of Work site (www.standards.dfes.gov.uk/schemes3). As a trainee, you quickly come to both love and loathe the QCA Schemes of Work. They are to be loathed because in many schools they are all the planning – for every subject bar literacy and numeracy they offer a complete breakdown of what should be taught at each stage of each year. Following a simple dropdown menu, you can see that, for example, Unit 4 in history for Year 2 children concerns Florence Nightingale. Lesson One looks at who she was, and subsequent lessons focus on the Crimean War and why we should remember her. It is not necessary to have any real knowledge of the topic yourself as a teacher. By using the QCA Schemes all the teacher need do is follow the prescribed lessons.

But love or loathe the QCA Schemes, there is no getting away from them. From what I saw in schools, there are subject coordinators who see their job as little more than printing out the QCA Schemes and handing them out to other teachers. This becomes the long-term planning for the subject and so the individual teachers have no choice but to follow the lessons. The chances to go off on a tangent or investigate interesting points in depth are greatly limited as the coordinator is likely to see your success in terms of your ability to keep up with the QCA timetable.

Literacy and numeracy, already subdivided into the NLS and NNS, tend to be broken down in similar detail to the QCA. The numeracy site (www.standards.dfes.gov.uk/numeracy) includes a complete set of lessons for every topic, and while these are not used universally most schools will teach from some scheme or other, be it Heinemann, Medal Maths or Abacus. If you're expecting to walk into a classroom with your own agenda and your own ideas then I'm afraid you are in for a bit of a shock.

But although you may have to stay within the framework there are at least some great lessons ideas out there. Your university library will be chock full of lazy student-friendly books such as *100 Year 5 Maths Lessons* and *The Complete Year One Teacher* but I preferred some of the online resources where benevolent teachers post little gems of ideas for free. One such site is the Teacher Resource Exchange (http://tre.ngfl.gov.uk/), but by far my favourite, and not just because it was built by a tutor on my course, is the Primary Teacher's Toolbox (www.btinternet.com/~tony.poulter/). If you put up with the God-awful music on every page – I won't spoil the surprise, but you will recognize, and hate the homepage song within one hundredth of a second of it starting – it is a site that boasts pretty much all you will need: carefully selected links to other sites, suggested resources, lessons and games and endless little extras that you will love finding (if you plan on building a school website all the resources you will need are here).

Finally, there are two absolute essentials that trainees, and no other teacher, must bear in mind with regard to planning.

Always write out a full lesson plan – when your folders are checked you will get into no end of trouble if you neglected to write a plan, arguing that you knew it in your head or that you thought the longer term or weekly plans were enough. Assessors are sticklers for such detail. If your plans are printed and in order, they will love you. Show any sign of disorganization and they'll have you for dinner. In their eyes being a bad planner is akin to being a bad teacher.

And finally finally, make sure you include a plenary. In lessons you observe you will probably see a plenary once every ten lessons, but you must do as the teacher says, not as they do. The plenary can be a show and tell of what pupils have achieved in the lesson, it can set homework or it can set a few slightly harder challenges. It doesn't really matter what is in it as long as it ties in to what you have taught, but just make sure it goes in. If you want to find out why you need to include one just try missing one out when you're being assessed . . .

# 33 Darling, pretend you're a tree

At primary school I was what might now be known as a geek. Although reasonably popular in class and blessed with the Gary Linekar-like ability of being able to score the winning goal in football, I worked too hard to be one of the cool kids. Inconceivable as it may be to those who know me now, I was never happier than when charging through mathematics homework, writing a story for English or just striving to boost my reading age to 13 by learning words such as puberty, menstruation and hormonal.

Stress came with the 'fun' subjects. My artwork, as ten rejection letters from Tony Hart's Gallery would suggest, was a disaster; In home economics my dishes tended to finish up bright red due to shoddy knifemanship; and the end product of music lessons was always a tune resembling a slowed-down version of 'Frere Jaques'.

Twenty or so years later, I still have the same problems. My cooking, with two dishes mastered (spaghetti Bolognese and chilli con carne), might have progressed in leaps and bounds but I'm still just as hopeless at art and music. Actually, that's a lie. I'm worse. Because of this, the lectures in these subjects have generally been quite stressful. I have no problems teaching art, after all half the battle is just inspiring the class to be creative, but being told by your tutor that all you need to be able to draw a life-like rendering of a galloping horse's face is a little more concentration is a tad galling. Concentration isn't the problem, lack of talent is – I could spend hours studying a stick man and still draw him out of proportion.

There was, however, one subject I was dreading even more than art. Drama. The thought of pretending to be a squirrel gathering nuts, or a tree in bloom doesn't really get my juices flowing. It seemed that all my worst fears would be realized when the lesson started with us passing an imaginary stone around a circle before doing silly walks around the room while describing our favourite room (I'm ashamed to say it's the toilet in my case).

But, unlike all those years ago, it was actually both inspiring and entertaining. Inspiring because it showed just how valuable a tool drama can be in boosting pupils' creativity and confidence, and entertaining because it's not every day you get to see a roomful of adults making fools (for want of a better word) of themselves. I put it down to the fact that while the course may be hard work it's still infinitely better than doing a nine to five job, sitting in meetings and having to suck up to the boss. From September the real work will start so the time on the course is to be enjoyed. Give me a choice between hours of planning or doing a mime and I'd choose the latter. Probably.

What's even more interesting is how the people, or at least some of the people, on the course seem to take up the roles you could imagine them taking in class. There are the talkers, the fidgeters, the quiet ones, the teacher's pets and the cheeky pupils. Sadly, well not all that sadly as none of the groups seem that appealing, I'm pretty sure that I have a tendency to sneak into the latter group. Sitting in a classroom writing a poem, playing numeracy games or composing a tune on the glockenspiel is frankly amusing and when you think about what you could be doing – writing a report, filing expenses, catching the tram to work – it's impossible not to chuckle.

Whether all the cheeky chappies should be combined is another matter entirely. Last week in drama our group had the task of producing a simple news report and, instead, launched into a three-minute comedy sketch, complete with 30-second delays caused by an imaginary dodgy radio link between the studio and on-the-spot reporter. The other groups all did fairly straight-laced reports, however the common theme between us all was that we had completed the objective, been creative in doing so, and had also injected some of our own personality.

Our group went for the humorous approach, an approach I imagine we'll all maintain when teaching full time. It's not a style favoured by all, many teachers seem to see humour and education as being uneasy bedfellows, but my ethos will be to learn through having fun. If the class want to write funny stories then all well and good. If they use the odd rude word, all the better. In one class I observed, a young lad wrote a brilliant story but the only feedback he got was negative because he had used an 'inappropriate word' for bottom. Such feedback could stifle his creativity, discourage him from taking risks and lead to him writing in a more prosaic style just to please the teacher. In my class I want the pupils to write to please themselves first and me second. Put it the other way round and, to use an 'inappropriate word', it's the pupils getting a bum deal.

# 34  Racial intolerance

One of the best things about living in a modern, liberal democracy is that everyone of schooling age is entitled to a free education. One of the worst things about living in Britain is that there are many people who would seemingly like this reversed.

Incredible as it might seem, there is a large group of people – I believe they are called racists – who would like Britain to turn back the years. To about 1869, prior to the first (and there have been many) *Education Act*. Of course, they would phrase it in their own inimitable style. 'We don't want 'em here', 'They're not welcome' or 'I won't have my kid sitting next to one of them'. The group being referred to in each case are travellers – the minority group it is seemingly still ok to loathe without fear of censure.

Travellers and gypsies (gypsies tending to be Anglo-Saxon, travellers Irish) have the same rights as everyone else, and yet somehow those rights don't seem to apply. Which other group would find a deputy head teacher refusing them a place in school purely on terms of race? Would parents tell teachers that their children weren't to mix with any other group? Would a solicitor joke about the genocide of any other group, stating 'there was only one person who had an answer to this gypsy problem and that was Hitler'?

Unsurprisingly, the fact that travellers risk constant overt racial abuse every time they go to school tends to put them off going. Their attendance rate, especially in high school, is shockingly low, but then perhaps that's not too surprising given the sort of abuse meted out from fellow pupils. An eight-year-old was sent a Christmas card in the school post that read 'f--k off you f---ing gypsy'. At another school, three out of the four travellers enrolled were forced out within weeks. The other stayed, but only after lying to convince everyone that she was Indian and not a traveller. They got off lightly though. Fifteen-year-old Johnny Delaney was kicked to death by

local youths in Ellesmere Port. Despite one of the youths shouting
'he deserves it, he's only a gypsy' as he jumped on his head, the attack
was not deemed to be racist. The case, unlike any other I can think
of involving youths killing another youngster, failed to make the
front pages.

Perhaps, and I'm just speculating, after writing stories that
Britain would be 'swamped' by travellers from Eastern Europe following the expansion of the EU, Johnny's case didn't quite tie in
with the editorial bias of our right-wing press. Incidentally, local
councils report that there has been no increase in numbers coming
from Eastern Europe since the expansion – apparently people aren't
all that keen to leave beautiful Prague to come and sign on here.

As a teacher I will be happy to integrate travellers into my classroom. I recall my own school days when members of a travelling
circus would come for a few weeks at a time. They brought a new
perspective, were exciting to talk to and were universally popular,
perhaps in part due to the free tickets they'd give out. However,
I will only be able to do so much. There are so many adults who
need re-educating, but where to start? Should it be with the great
and good of a local community who decided to torch a mock-up
gypsy caravan complete with models of gypsy children on Bonfire
Night? How about the solicitor who, in defending a well-heeled
shoplifter, said 'this is not some gypsy from some part of
Czechoslovakia who has come here on the make to go into our
stores to steal with a gang.' Finally, there's the parent who filled in
the section of a school form asking for suggested improvements
with 'get rid of the gypsy children'.

I find it all so depressing. As a trainee teacher you like to feel that
you can make a difference, you won't be changing the world, but
you might help a few hundred kids grow up the right way. If they're
going to be filled with racist filth at home and, worse still go to a
school with racist staff, then the influence of one right-minded
teacher will probably be negligible. In any case there's not even
much time for the teacher to work on any correcting of the misconceptions. There's ten hours of literacy and numeracy a week to
be fitted in, not to mention endless ICT, design technology and
singing practice. Small matters like tolerance and growing up not
to be a racist bigot will just have to be left to chance.

# 35 Oi! Get off my land

The one thing all trainee teachers moan about (when I say the one thing I'm temporarily forgetting the kids' behaviour, the poor pay, the fall in respect for the profession, the stress and the sheer fact that you might not always feel like putting on a show for 30 disillusioned kids) is the planning. And, like all other trainees, I too hate all the planning. So there we have it, column over for this week.

Well, perhaps not quite. I do dislike the planning, but it's not the obvious planning that really gets my goat. Planning all aspects of all lessons is a necessary evil, at least for trainee teachers, otherwise you go to school certain that each lesson will prove to be a massive cock-up and are then proved absolutely right. Being naturally efficient in movement, if not quite lazy, it's sometimes tempting to have an evening off to watch the football with a beer rather than plan a lesson on algorithms. It's not a wise move though. Keeping a couple of children occupied for even 10 minutes is a hard enough task – keeping 33 occupied for six hours would be a prospect certain to cause a nervous fit if there was any time after all the planning to actually think about it. Actually, I've just started thinking about it now. Christ, that's depressing . . .

Planning lessons is therefore a necessary evil (or a welcome chance to plan a series of engaging tasks for your class of cherubs, depending on who you talk to). Planning for other adults, however, is an ache in the nether regions.

In my former life as a journalist, I rarely even had to plan for myself. I'd roll in to work at 9.07am, check emails for an hour or so, browse a few websites, write a few thousand words entirely different from the day before's words, have a lengthy lunch, have a lengthy break, browse a bit more and then disappear to the pub at 4.57pm.

I accepted that as a teacher I'd have to plan for myself and obviously plan the lessons. What I'd failed to consider was planning for the other adults. Schools nowadays, unlike when I's a lad and the harangued teacher could go a whole career (usually about two terms) without seeing any form of support, are full of support staff. There's the TAs – teaching assistants – though Territorial Army might be more appropriate in some schools; learning assistants, specialist staff for children with educational or behavioural special needs; specialist staff for children for whom English is an additional language; and specialist staff to help the specialist staff.

It's no exaggeration to say that the Human Resources manager at ICI has a quieter life than whoever sorts out the payroll at your local school. Actually, it's massive exaggeration, ICI employ 33,000 people, whereas a school employs far fewer. Certainly no more than 31,500.

The point I'm making, laboriously, is that it's not easy to find things for these people to do. Admittedly, some just get on with it, their remit is to work with specific children. Most though work from the teacher's plans. It means that lessons have to be good as, otherwise, you have an unimpressed witness or two as the class descends into chaos. I'm convinced it was easier for teachers in the past – they could die a private death away from the prying eyes of more experienced colleagues.

The natural tendency, and it's one I'm guilty of at times, is to simply put the TAs with the more unruly pupils to stop any trouble before it arises. I'm not entirely sure that this is what they are really in the class for, but it does have its advantages. Using the TA in this way frees up the teacher to work with other pupils and also limits the number of disruptions to the lesson, thus ensuring a better quality of education for all.

There is, though, a counter argument and, being in essay mode having given in 5,000 words of waffle in the past week, I've decided to include it for reasons of balance. The theory goes that it is unfair on the other pupils, the badly behaved actually benefiting as they get to work in small groups with an adult all the time and so have more of their questions and queries answered. Fortunately I'm not fully in essay mode and so don't feel forced to come to a conclusion based on limited reading and a few half-developed ideas pinched from academics.

I don't know what the best way to use TAs is, though a radical option might be to ask them what they'd feel most suited to or how their skills might be best utilized.

Another option might be just to have fewer of them. It's unlikely to happen, but most trainees I've discussed the subject with (one) would happily forgo TAs altogether. Having someone else in your classroom, however good they are, acts as a barrier and stops you from being quite yourself as a teacher. As a trainee it makes you feel watched – the TA has probably been there for years and could take great delight in highlighting your shortcomings to an eager staffroom.

A classroom without TAs would allow the teacher to relax and actually grow in confidence knowing that the buck really did stop with them. It would also, though you realize this is only a minor point, allow them to show *Finding Nemo* on a Friday afternoon when they have nothing else planned.

# 36 Placement two

Well done for getting this far! As you'll already know, many people on the course drop out long before the second placement so just making it this far is an achievement in itself. Unfortunately, it isn't an achievement worth very much, but at least it means you're not a lilly-livered quitter. Getting this far won't guarantee you a job or even passing the course. It doesn't really even mean that you are cut out to be a teacher (though I'm sure that you are). All it means is that, at this stage, you are in good shape.

The past, at this stage, really does not count for all that much. It is brilliant if you have passed tasks with flying colours, better still if you have tonnes of standards, and truly wonderful if you already feel confident in the classroom and feel like a fully fledged teacher. Equally, the trainees who have struggled and are lagging behind some of their peers are not actually all that far behind at all. The knowledge already acquired at this stage is invaluable, but the tasks passed are largely irrelevant. For all trainees it is the second placement that is absolutely crucial to the whole course. This is because, within reason, it really does not matter what level you achieve in your first placement. The primary aim of the early part of the course is to bring everyone up to a reasonable level. At the end of the first placement, some students will have passed most of the standards, others very few. Some might even have a job lined up, whereas others will be some way from having the confidence even to apply. These differences are totally natural, the result of differing levels of pre-course experience and different levels of help in the first placement school.

However, from these vastly different starting points going into the second placement, everyone has to leave at the same level. All the standards must be achieved, the final report must be passed and, most importantly of all, the student must either have a job or have a plan as to how they are going to get one or what they are going to do if they don't.

On top of this there will almost inevitably be demands placed on your time in the form of dreaded course tasks. If it's any consolation the deadline for these should be early on in the placement, so at least you don't go into the final weeks having to teach 80 per cent of lessons, concentrate on standards, apply for jobs, go for interviews and also have to plan and write an essay.

As with the first placement, time in school starts with a series of day visits. Here, with the benefit of hindsight from placement one, I made sure that I wasn't overly friendly with the class and I also got to grips with the pupils' names a lot more quickly. A simple mental challenge I set myself was to pick a pupil at random and then think what their name was – after a couple of days of this I had them all remembered perfectly.

The fact that in a few weeks you will be teaching everything also acts as a great motivator at this stage, and only the most blasé of students would consider wasting any spare time when they could be checking out resources or starting to plan units of work.

After this initial easy start, the placement becomes all action. Whereas in placement one you teach for a maximum of 60 per cent of the time in any week, and across the whole placement probably only teach for a quarter of the time in school, in placement two you take much more responsibility. For the first time, the trainee feels like the class's actual teacher rather than someone who stands in for the odd lesson. What this means is that there is no real let-up. From the start of each week until the end, you will have the responsibility of teaching all the lessons, so unlike placement one it won't be a case of getting through a lesson with a sense of relief and then relaxing for an hour. You get through a lesson, if you're lucky run off for a quick cup of tea, and then teach another lesson. Paradoxically, I found that teaching more regularly actually became a lot less stressful than teaching occasional lessons in placement one. Through teaching more regularly you build up a far better rapport with the class (aided of course by the fact that you've got some experience and a wealth of reading behind you at this stage) and also stop worrying about each lesson in isolation. The lessons start becoming part of a coherent whole of learning and as a teacher you can start making links between the different subjects.

Far more importantly, taking so many lessons means that you can try out all those little strategies on behaviour management, planning and assessment that you've read about and start deciding which ones you'll implement in your own classroom, hopefully from September. And another huge benefit of being the class's main teacher, if only for a few weeks, is that you feel like a far more integral part of the school. Whether it is in assembly, in sports matches or on school trips, you actually start feeling like a member of staff rather than the work experience kid.

These benefits are secondary, however. The most important thing about the placement is that trainees get what they need out of it. This can be very different from the first placement when it is possible to not really know what you want to get from it – I went in having only spent around a month in schools as pre-course experience, none of this teaching, and so the first few weeks were a real eye-opener where I didn't really know what to expect or, at times, do. This is common of the first placement, but on finishing it, and with time to reflect back in college and, most importantly find out what other people got from the placement, the second placement should be approached with a far more detailed plan. My own plan included the standards I needed to hit, although these should be hit naturally just through teaching so much more, and also plans to improve my planning and assessment. For planning, I wanted to reach a stage whereby I was scheduling whole coherent units rather than disparate lessons. For assessment, having seen almost none of it in the first placement, I first wanted to catch up by learning about the methods used in school and then start introducing my own strategies.

A final aim was to stay on top of the dreaded files. In the first placement I'd tended to update them the night before someone actually wanted to look at them. In placement two I used the first few days in school to collect all the background information and then updated this as I went along. With the amount of other work you'll be doing, the last thing you'll want is to have to be sifting through Ofsted reports the night before the course assessor comes in.

But the second placement is about so much more than just staying on top of everything. In placement one, it feels as if you're a plate spinner, trying desperately to keep them all going, watching in horror as some start crashing around your ankles. In the second placement everything should come together and, rather than feeling like a thousand different tasks, things should start linking in with each other. For instance, plans should include assessment opportunities and the assessment should then be used to inform future plans. In the first placement this happens at a very basic level, often feeling like an extra chore that won't actually be used. In placement two it becomes essential as you realize that assessment actually makes the teaching easier, it highlights what you need to focus on in future lessons. I believe that the official term for the enlightenment at the end of the course is *The Usual Suspects* syndrome. Only towards the end does it make any sense, and even then there are a few gaping holes and bits which, on closer inspection, don't make any sense whatsoever (the need to spend two hours composing a dance, hours spent learning about interactive whiteboards when they were about as common as a virgin in a Swansea nightclub in the schools I went to, and the purpose of a course day out to a bookshop).

Starting to plan great lessons and hitting standards is, of course, only half the battle. The second placement is a chance to really start engaging with the whole life of the school – and not just to get that standard ticked off. As you engage more with the class and school as a whole it is natural to want a fuller role, usually through taking a more active role with school clubs. With my forte being sport (well sport, writing and browsing the Internet, but two of those don't make for particularly good clubs – especially in the height of summer), I plumped for helping out with rounders.

Rounders, for those of you who have forgotten, is the most English of sports. Baseball without the aggression, or even the need to make contact with the ball. Helping out with the club was a great chance to spend a few hours in the sunshine, see the pupils in a different light, with some of the less gifted in the classroom getting a real chance to shine, and also to impress with my ability to throw a ball a very long way (well, relatively, at least). It was also a great eye-opener to see the competitiveness of other schools, teachers and parents.

In a friendly rounders match, surely the least competitive sports match imaginable, I helped umpire a game and was amazed to see that the umpire from the other school, in charge because it was on their patch and also because I was 'only a trainee', had a rather bizarre counting system. Our school got 25 balls and had only two of their four rounders recorded. Their school got 33 balls and had 3 of their two rounders recorded. That they won was the biggest sporting scandal since Giovanni Evangelisti was awarded a long jump bronze medal at the 1987 Rome World Championships thanks to a judge who added 50 centimetres onto his mark. Sorry, obscure sports reference creeping in.

At the start of the course the second placement will loom like a black cloud. Up to 10 weeks spent away from college, in an alien classroom with, potentially, your entire future resting on the outcome. And if it was anything like that it would be terrible, but honestly it isn't. The second placement is actually the best time of the whole course. From learning so much through lectures and essays and reflecting on what went right and what went wrong from the first placement you will go into it as an infinitely better teacher than you were just a few months ago. By the time placement two comes around you can already teach a decent lesson; if you couldn't you would not have passed placement one, so this becomes a chance to shine. The second placement is not a problem, it is an opportunity. It is the release following the steamy build-up of the course, it is a parent taking the stabilizers off your bike and pushing you down a hill, it is finally asking out the girl you've fancied from afar for years and it is getting your A-level results after weeks of anxious waiting. It's all these clichés and more because it is your time. Your time to show what you have learnt and your time to prove you can teach.

# 37 Work creation scheme

For a recent essay, I wrote, or at least I think I wrote (17 cups of coffee and a marathon stint of online poker having taken their toll), that PE is a hard subject to assess. As theories go it wasn't anything too special. Chomsky probably contributed more to education in suggesting that, rather than learning by example, children have an innate ability to master complex grammatical structure, but it beat my previous essay musings that 'all things considered, Neville Chamberlain was a bit lilly-livered'.

The essay, subtitled 'How to state the bleeding obvious', looked at whether it's possible to measure achievement in areas as subjective as free-form dance. Over 3,000 words I suggested that it was pretty hard to assess PE, in fact I suggested this several hundred times, and to hammer the point home that little bit more I played my part in a group presentation on the same subject.

Why do I mention this? Well it's partly because, as with the essay, my mouse is constantly flitting over to 'Tools/Word count' in the hope that by rabbiting on I'll get somewhere near my target. It's the same strategy as used by kids in my current class who, in finding that they are 60 words short of their extended write target, throw in 60 more words seemingly (actually, in some cases) at random.

A more edifying reason is that my essay has been proved right in the last couple of weeks. Our PE lessons at present see the class squirming awkwardly when asked to hold hands with members of the opposite sex in that 1870s throwback that is country dancing. Of all the things I could have ended up teaching in PE (and I have coached cricket, tennis and football) this is by far the worst – to my mind it has no more place in a games lesson than chess – but that's a rant for another day (next week, perhaps).

Country dancing, for the blessed uninitiated, sees kids (although adults, probably the same ones who go line dancing, apparently do it as well) bumping into each other to what is essentially the same tune played at 16 different speeds. Dances are called things like Cumberland Sausage, the Oxo Cube and Dodosido, and the four moves are swing aimlessly, gallop randomly, squirm as if the girl next to you has an electric-shock buzzer in her hand and, by far the most common, pretend to be a dodgem. Watching it, you are reminded of GCSE science lessons, looking at the movement of gas particles in a vacuum. Indeed, view it with the music off and you might imagine that the class are being controlled by a particularly vindictive string puppeteer.

Amidst all this chaos the teacher should, at least theoretically, be assessing. Personally, the only sort of assessment I'd consider doing in this sort of lesson is the risk type as galloping bodies collide, but the current thinking that 'if it moves it must be assessed, categorized and filed' deems that trees are wasted in making entirely pointless notes.

The question is where to begin and what to assess. How can you tell anything about coordination when you have 33 nine- and ten-year-olds throwing each other around the hall? Equally, the chances of working out who has the rhythm to move in time with the music are somewhere less than zero given that the music seems to bear little resemblance to the prescribed moves (if moves isn't too grand a term for what are merely variations of embarrassed swings).

Every experienced teacher I have met gets around the problem in a tried and tested manner – namely they don't bother assessing PE, or for that matter, many of the 'foundation' subjects (those that aren't deemed as important as mathematics, English or science). That method, potential employers please stop reading now, is probably the one I'll favour too. The problem is that while on the course the trainee is charged with doing lots of things that they'll instantly drop once working properly.

Chief among these is build up tonnes of assessment material to make your files look good. Obviously assessment is important, but the need to assess every pupil's achievement in every lesson, as well as review your own practice in the lesson and how it could be improved and, on top of this, keep weekly logs of your time and progress against key issues, isn't necessarily what you need when you're up until gone midnight planning in any case.

But perhaps that is the main point of the course. To show that life as a teacher is work, work, work so you better get used to it now.

Why else would they set essay and presentation deadlines a couple of days before you're in school for eight weeks, thus tying up valuable planning time. And why else would they make you assess things that they must know you won't be assessing come September. It could only be for one of two reasons: either to make you hugely unpopular in school as you go in with an arm-long to do list, or to prepare you for the 40-year hard slog that is a teaching career.

Assuming it's the second reason, then the course leaders are to be thanked. Life is hard, so get used to it – it's an uplifting message for teachers the world over to pin up on their class walls. All it took to get the message across was a well-timed essay and an overwhelming booklet called the School-Based Training Nightmare and, in my case, $27 net loss on online poker during said essay-writing session. That, I'm sure you'll agree, is a price well worth paying.

# 38 Damned with faint praise

In teaching there are numerous things that hopefully I'll never get fully used to: putting sand on fresh piles of vomit, sitting down to six separate piles of books to mark, showdowns with angry parents and, most of all, having someone in my classroom assessing me.

It is a phenomenon that teaching shares with few other professions, having someone there watching your every move, presenting the calm face of indifference as they tick the little boxes on their flip chart. It's certainly strange following on from my former career when anyone watching me would have been fairly unimpressed by my mediocre output and regular breaks for bacon butties. To be honest I'd have gone to pieces if someone was looking over my shoulder, I'm one of those people who won't even read aloud what they've written so I'd have been mortified and rendered somewhat impotent if there was a man in a suit (men in suits being a rarity in online journalism, as indeed are remotely smart men) looming.

At least, though, I'd have been fairly confident that I was good at my job. In teaching, although decent and certainly not the worst teacher ever, I'm hardly the finished article after only a few weeks in school and so having an assessor in is doubly worrying. But like death, and only slightly more welcome, the assessor comes and his coming for me was earlier this week.

The first thing he does, and here I learnt a valuable lesson, is to check your files. Regulars of this column might have picked up on the fact that I'm not much of a files person – I have them, they have the requisite bits of paper stuffed in somewhere, but they are not my main priority. Last time he came for a brief visit they were, to put it frankly, a tad messy. The order was all askew, sections that should have been present were still located on my hard drive and there was a tea stain all over my RE medium-term plan. This time, the paper was whiter, the files newer and, crème de la crème, packed full of labelled dividers. The assessor was impressed – a few cursory checks later and he gave them the green light. Evidently, if you can be bothered to go to Smiths and buy a jumbo pack of coloured file dividers you are sufficiently efficient for a career in teaching.

Notwithstanding (not a word I'd usually use, but the class has been looking at connectives . . . ) the file success, the main challenge remained: teaching a lesson worthy of the assessor's equivalent of a thumbs up. A gruff handshake perhaps. One thing that was certain was that gushing praise was out of the question. The report sheet we get back has two options: 'Satisfactory' and 'At Risk'. Being dammed with faint praise is the best the trainee can hope for, while 'At Risk' remains ambiguous. Who is at risk? The trainee who faces 40 years in a profession they may be manifestly unsuited to, or the children who could go uneducated for a year?

Playing it fairly safe, I chose a lesson based on writing a newspaper-style report though with the slightly anti-establishment headline of 'Rats close school'. Brazenly I hadn't done any extra planning for the lesson, fearing the old adage about the best-laid plans of rats and men and also figuring that it's best not to worry too much about such things. Fortunately the laissez faire attitude worked a treat. The class were perfectly behaved, answered the questions and worked hard. I must have looked like a proper teacher.

In fact it went so well that I actually knew it was going well and so wasn't remotely worried about the debrief. A satisfactory mark beckoned – halcyon days indeed. The assessor was suitably impressed, even giving some contraband real praise by whispering 'good' lesson, though if you asked him he'd have to deny it vehemently.

The effect has been marked. Where before I'd spent hours agonizing over every lesson, now I have the ability to plan lessons quickly and the confidence to stick with my first instinct. More importantly, it has made me feel like a proper teacher and with that I finally have the confidence to start really looking for a job.

When the assessor arrived, it was a moment to dread, yet ironically it has turned out to be a watershed as if I can deliver in front of him then I must be halfway decent. I'm not about to change my initial thoughts, I still don't want to have to get used to constant assessment of my performance, but I'll concede that on this occasion it was a good thing. All I need to do now is keep the chant going. 'I'm satisfactory, I'm satisfactory, I'm satisfactory.' Praise doesn't come much higher.

# 39 Hunting for a needle in a haystack

The sharp-eyed among you will have noticed that the last few columns have been painfully short of details relating to my struggle to find employment. There is a good reason for this – there are no jobs going within 30 miles of my house.

Like most people starting a PGCE course, I had assumed that getting a job would present the least of my problems. After all, why would the Government, in all its infinite wisdom, throw money at people to persuade them to train for a profession that was fast-becoming saturated with too many trainees. The sharp-eyed (who could really just skip straight to the next column at this stage) will already know the answer – the Government's knowledge is anything but infinite. It's probably not even finite as that would imply a beginning. Ten years ago, perhaps fewer still, there was a genuine shortage of teachers, now there is merely an imbalance. If you fancy teaching maths in London you'll walk into a job (you probably don't even need to bother training – just turn up saying you've worked on a till or something). If you fancy primary teaching in a big city you should be ok, but if you fancy teaching out in the sticks – the sort of job where you can forsake body armour – you may be in for a big disappointment.

With the course over and the supposed glut of jobs having failed to materialize, somewhere around half the people on the course have found employment. That statistic in itself does not sound too great, but when you consider that those who have found work are generally the people who are willing to relocate it becomes even worse. For those of us unable to simply upsticks to London, Birmingham or Liverpool because of mortgages, partners' work, children or other commitments – pub-quiz teams, mistresses, that sort of thing – the prospects are grim. A couple of weeks ago I went to look around a school 30 miles from my house, then a few days later I looked around another school 20 miles from home in the opposite direction. On both trips I saw the same four people from my course. Neither of the schools was particularly appealing, the jobs were only temporary and we'd all have at least a 40-mile round trip but we all felt obliged to go. There wasn't anything else in the offing.

Eventually I decided not to apply for the first school. The atmosphere was exactly how I've always imagined a Victorian sweathouse to feel, the facilities were awful (try teaching ICT when it's one computer per four pupils) and the staff seemed about as motivated as I would be if working for the Barrow-in-Furness tourist board. I knew instantly that if I took a job there I would have left in disgust within a year, probably a term, and turned my back on teaching for good. In the words of BA Barrackas 'I pity the fool who took that job.'

The second school looked slightly more promising. The job was for a Year 4 class, the same age as I had been teaching on placement. The head was welcoming and the pupils, from what I saw, seemed pretty well-behaved. Of course, you can't really gauge the pupils in the space of a short visit, but at least they weren't pouring petrol onto the furniture. What impressed me most about the school were the facilities. Every classroom had an interactive whiteboard, there were scores of computers, a well-stocked library and the sports hall looked like something the LA Lakers should be playing on. It was easily the best-equipped school I've seen in Cheshire – a fact not entirely unrelated to it being maintained and funded by the church instead of the local education authority.

However there is a major downside to church-maintained schools – especially if you aren't a practising Christian yourself. The governors tend to take a dim view of agnostics – they'd probably burn them in assembly given the chance – and, judging from the feedback I got from one school, a terrible Christian teacher is often preferable to a brilliant non-believer. Apparently it's to do with the school ethos – the ethos seeming to be that 'we'll appoint church-goers no matter what'. The attitude of the governors appears to be based on fear, a fear that spending one year under the influence of someone who doesn't devote his Sundays to worship will turn their children from God-fearing angels into anarchic monsters.

Frankly it seems very sad – I'd want my children to be able to develop their own beliefs based on knowledge rather than indoctrination, but there you go. What I really wish is that I'd known just how important my religious beliefs would be before applying for the job.

On walking round the school, the head reassured me that there was no need to be religious, merely to teach in a manner sympathetic to the school ethos. It turns out that what she actually meant was that religious beliefs were unimportant as long as another key criteria was met – namely that no practising Christian bothered applying for the job.

Believe it or not, I can get over the school's decision. Afterall, even if it had been a state-maintained school there's absolutely no guarantee that I'd have got the job. Equally, the prospect of a 30-mile drive along notoriously busy roads each morning wasn't all that appealing.

What really annoys me is the belief that because someone bothers going to church once a week they are made of stronger moral fibre. If school is about anything then it is about preparing youngsters for living in a world full of different faiths, points of view and religions. Given the situation in the world today where religious intolerance costs thousands of lives a year, might it not be an idea to give children equal exposure to all religions so that they can make their own choices out of knowledge and respect. The doctrine of blind loyalty might have its place on the terraces, but should be ousted from the classrooms and from governors' tick lists in scrutinizing would-be employees.

# 40 A little respect

Clearly I have too much time on my hands at present for, in today's column, I will strive to answer one of the great questions of our age, namely, why do children no longer have any respect for – well pretty much anything or anyone?

One hundred years ago children were seen but not heard (and they were only actually seen if you bothered looking directly up a chimney flume), 50 years ago they sat respectfully through the dullest of mathematics lessons, thanks in no small part to the swishing cane, and ten years ago, though they may have been demotivated, they were at least pretty quiet. Nowadays, children are violent, drug-addicted louts only interested in setting a new world record for the number of ASBOs collected. Obviously I exaggerate – even our judges are reluctant to give ASBOs to primary school kids – but the question still stands; ask a random person their views on the youth of today (please don't ask anyone drooling at the mouth) and watch them turn into Victor Meldrew.

In fact, I suggest you play a little game involving a checklist and pencil. Ask people for their views on youngsters and then tick off the clichéd phrases you hear – 'No respect', 'When I was a lad . . . ,' 'I don't feel safe on the streets at night', '. . . Hanging around street corners'. Admittedly it's not a very good game, there's no way of winning and it could lead to you being beaten up – ironically probably by someone who had respect drummed into them at school – but it at least passes the time if you find yourself with six hours to kill in a random city (as I did in Liverpool yesterday, but that's a whole other story – suffice it to say that 10 years was not quite long enough for me to arrange getting a new passport).

The one idea that will be rammed home mercilessly is that children's behaviour is getting worse and, sadly, it's a view that seems entirely accurate. Turn on any news report and you'll hear a story about a youth committing an awful crime. Go into any school and you won't have to wait too long before seeing a teacher openly disrespected by a pupil. From this it would seem to be natural to conclude that children themselves are getting worse and so, being a bleeding heart liberal, being contrary and being someone who needs to expand this column, I'm going to argue the opposite. Children's behaviour may be getting worse, but children themselves are the same as they ever were. The difference now is that they get away with so much and, most importantly, they know that they will get away with the pranks they get up to.

Go back 50 years and corporal punishment was being dealt out with a certain degree of relish up and down the country and it wasn't just the cane handing out punishment. Children were hit with slippers, rulers and any other solid object to hand, while some teachers even took sadistic delight in devising their own punishments – being lifted off the ground by the sideburns being among the most painful. It's fair to assume that the children at the time were just as prone towards misbehaving – why else would there be a need for punishments – it is just that the prospect of being brought to tears was enough to discourage all bar the most suicidal of miscreants.

Jumping forward to my own schooldays, corporal punishment may have gone (though I was once hit in the eye by a piece of chalk chucked by the teacher) but all that served to do was to make teachers more creative in their sanctions. At primary school, forgetting swimming trunks meant going into the pool in your pants and then having to keep them on for the rest of the day. Writing with a sideways slant meant having to write 'I am not a crab' 500 times.

At secondary school I once committed the mortal sin of chewing a mint during class and was duly punished by being made to run round the school field five times. Not too bad, you might think until you realize that this was in winter, it was snowing, I was forced to wear my PE kit and there were older kids lining up to throw snowballs at me.

All these punishments, though off the cuff, were highly effective. As a pupil you realized that if you broke even the most trivial of rules there was a devilish punishment waiting. Sin in haste, repent at leisure. The teachers could not all command respect, but they could at least command good behaviour if only through fear of reprisal.

Nowadays, while the level of respect is probably much the same, the level of disobedience is much higher and if you want my take on it, and even if you don't you're going to get it because this is my column, this is because children no longer fear the reaper. Or should that be fear the teacher.

I'm not suggesting (at least not in print) that children should be terrified of the consequences of any little step out of line, however I do feel that we might have gone a bit far the other way. Sanctions in schools are, to be frank, generally rubbish. Thanks to the system of reminders and warnings used in many schools, pupils are given a green light to get away with at least one piece of bad behaviour a day. Tell Johnny to shut his mouth in literacy and it's a reminder, push Ellie in the playground and it's a warning and, as long as they don't offend again, that's it for the day. No proper reprimand and a clean slate the following day.

And guess what – the following day the exact same thing happens and so in a typical week some of the pupils cunningly offend ten times and yet receive absolutely no punishment of note. I doubt I offended ten times in a typical year in primary school and yet I have vivid memories of swimming in my pants, being reduced to tears by the headmaster, writing lines and washing the playground (though I had written the word 'shit' in giant chalk letters, so that was perhaps fair).

Teachers nowadays have none of the power to administer ad hoc punishment and so it seems to me that their already tough job has been made far tougher. On the course, we are constantly told to avoid punishments that could in any way be deemed humiliating but, in reality, what does this leave? Being made to sit out playtime could be seen as humiliating, as could be a trip to another class for the afternoon. It's punishment after all, not holiday time. During my time at school I was forced to endure punishments that would no doubt be deemed somewhat humiliating and yet I bare absolutely no grudge towards the teachers concerned. I probably deserved it anyway and, in hindsight, I'd much rather take a few doses of harsh medicine than risk turning into a gobby lout.

# 41  A day to forget – or at least try to

Today was one of the most annoying days of my life so, rather than attempting to analyse it, I will instead recount all the messy blows.

4.30am   Woken up by cat's 'friendly' play – namely scratching at my eyes and gnawing at my wrists.

4.50am   Feed cat, discover that I now look like a heroin addict thanks to cat's scratching of arms.

5.00am   Fall asleep again. Bliss.

5.30am   Woken by alarm clock – time to get up as I'm getting a lift in with my wife and she has to be in work at some ridiculous hour.

6.00am   Having washed (quickly), done teeth and got dressed, I cut a neat triangle out of the base of my nose with razor and watch in dim bewilderment as the basin turns crimson.

6.07am   Leave house looking like a papier-mâché man, copious amounts of toilet paper hanging from my nose.

6.30am   Arrive in town where I am to have a job interview, only with one problem. I am two and a half hours early. Walk to supermarket.

6.45am   Walk away from supermarket having discovered that it doesn't open until 8am. Quicken step as first drops of rain fall.

7.02am   Arrive at gents toilets. With nothing better to do, stay there for 80 minutes playing mini golf on my mobile.

8.20am   Start walk to school. This turns out to be somewhat quicker than anticipated and so, at 8.30am I ponder how to kill more time.

8.50am   Having walked around the block four times (looking decidedly dodgy in the process), walk through school gates. Ring bell until . . .

9.03am   Someone opens the door. Am three minutes late for interview thanks to bone-idle secretary.

9.10am   Asked by head if I would like a drink. Request a tea, no sugar and get tea with several sugars. Drink it, narrowly avoiding retching, so as not to look rude (in hindsight consider this may have been some sort of pre-interview test of character).

9.20am   In classroom alone as parent walks in. Asked whether school trip is still on, I answer first thing that comes to head 'Yes, I think so'. In hindsight, possibly another mistake.

9.30am   Head, deputy head, head of Key Stage 2 and some governor or other walk in for interview. After formalities, head hands me a sheet which says something like: The key to good teaching is: a) Good subject knowledge, b) Good planning, c) Good assessment, d) Good working relationships with colleagues, e) Good motivational skills.

Head explains that the first task is to order these in terms of importance – I am to have ten minutes.

9.36am   Having spent six minutes rummaging through my mental thesaurus for alternatives to 'good', I start the task.

9.37   Having figured statistically that I have something like a one in seven billion chance of getting the right answer, I put down first order that seems reasonable.

9.39am   After two minutes thumb twiddling, I hastily reorder the list.

9.40am   Hand over list. My order is: good motivational skills, good subject knowledge, good planning, good assessment and, perhaps controversially, good working relationships with colleagues at the bottom.

9.42am   Start explaining the unexplainable, namely my order. Bizarrely I become incredibly lucid in interviews and I manage to chatter on for about half an hour – the thrust being that without being able to motivate your class you are doomed in any case as children that aren't motivated won't learn anything. Good subject knowledge comes next as this gives you the confidence to teach and also to go off on small tangents and answer any questions that may arise. Tied in to this is good planning and, in the planning provision should be made for assessment. My reasoning for putting working relationships last is that you could survive in teaching if you were brilliant in the classroom but a right git in the staffroom, whereas you couldn't if they were reversed.

10.15am   Governor starts one of those horrible role-play questions. 'If I was to walk into your classroom, what would I see?' she asks. Resist temptation to say either four walls, a ceiling and a door, or nothing – the lights are off.

10.18am    Notice smile on governor's face. She seems enchanted by my fake utopia full of displays, water fountains, Baroque music and oriental fan waivers.

10.20am    Deputy asks what I would do if faced by pupil who continually misbehaved. Scanning mental options, I quickly cast aside those such as throw him into the corridor, make him run round the field and pass him on to another teacher. A big exclamation mark appears above my head as I remember the warning system – say that I'd give him a reminder, then a warning and then maybe make him miss playtime or even ring his parents and invite them in for a chat.

10.24am    Head asks for my views on Mind Friendly Learning. Punch the air as have read up on this the night before. Talk about importance of seeing the bigger picture and tying disparate bits of learning into one another. Also, state the importance of refreshing the brain and body, be it through having water bottles on every table, plenty of fresh air, regular breaks for stretches and exercises and maybe even a bit of music in the background. Feeling in my element, I talk about the role of modern foreign language (MFL) guru Eva Hoffman and her use of mind mapping whereby you take a central starting topic and write down related topics. Think, but don't say, that this is merely a glorified name for spider charts.

10.35am    Head and the rest thank me for my time. Head asks whether I am still a firm candidate for role (I am). From their responses I can tell that it has gone well.

10.37am    Walk through school gates, unfasten tie, undo top button and stop holding beer belly in.

10.38am    Turn mobile back on, have to be ready for their call offering me the job.

10.40am    Practice response – will it be a cool 'Thank you, I'll have to discuss it with my partner' or, more likely, 'Really, you want me? I'll come straight back and sign – that way there's no way you can go back on the decision.'

10.45am    Arrive at bus stop in good time for the 10.48 service.

10.55am    Check timetable again. Notice that 10.48 service doesn't run on Tuesdays.

11.02am    Buy newspaper, chocolate bar and pen from shop.

11.10am   Back at bus stop, start Sudoko puzzle. It's an extra hard one – only one square is pre-filled.

11.17am   Give up on puzzle having tried, without success, to solve by putting numbers in at random.

11.25am   Phone rings, it's the school. Am amazed that they have rung so soon – they were interviewing all day. They must have told others not to bother after seeing me.

11.26am   Answer phone. Head starts by saying do you remember applying for job with us. Do I remember? The interview only finished an hour ago – resist urge to say 'I'm not bloody amnesiac.'

11.27am   Head says 'I'm sorry to inform you . . .' An odd start to a phone call offering someone a job. Perhaps she's been watching too much *Pop Idol* – I'm sorry to inform you that most of the people didn't get the job. However, you did!

11.29am   Nope, she hasn't been watching *Pop Idol* (I asked). She informs me that the job no longer exists – a teacher who had been off on long-term sick leave has decided that he'll be ok to return and so they don't need anyone for next year. My first thought is 'Bollocks. I didn't even ask for expenses.'

11.34am   Bus turns up at apparently random time – turns out it's the delayed 8.47am. Fare comes to £1.30, I hand over a tenner and get 70p change. 'Sorry guv, that's cleaned me out,' says driver.

11.38am   Read article on London buses in *G2* section of the *Guardian*. It includes a quote from Margaret Thatcher saying 'any man beyond the age of 26 who finds himself on a bus can consider himself a failure'.

11.50am   Alight bus. Step into muddy puddle. Step back and get splashed by car driving straight through same puddle.

11.57am   Buy *TES* on way home.

12.04pm   Check jobs in *TES*.

12.04pm   Finish checking jobs. There are exactly zero primary teaching jobs in Cheshire.

12.10pm   Cat gives me a welcome home in her own inimitable style by scratching and ruining my suit trousers.

12.12pm   Start writing column.

14.07pm   Accidentally turn off computer in attempting to plug television in.

14.10pm   After three minutes of profuse swearing restart column.

17.56pm   Enough's enough. End column.

# 42 The joy of stats

The very best thing about teaching primary school children is seeing their ambitions. In my class at present there is a lad who wants to become a scientist, a girl who fancies herself as an Olympic athlete, two potential brain surgeons, three wannabe astronauts and a lot of hopeful footballers. Pretty much everyone in the class already has a dream job, they are passionate about it and they are at an age when they could still all fulfil their dreams.

What none of them want to be, and indeed what no child in the world (or adult for that matter) should want to be, is a data analyst. Handling data – it's the devil's work and yet it is what I have found myself teaching all week.

Handling data is work that should only be carried out by people who cannot handle other humans. If you cannot bare any sort of interaction with other breathing mammals then go ahead, sit in front of a computer all day staring at numbers. If not, do something else.

Unfortunately it has to be done by someone. I don't know why it has to be done, but apparently it does. Computer systems all over the world are spewing out numbers and there have to be people on hand to analyse the data and make some sort of sense of it. Predicting the end of the world from temperature rises, working out how tall the average Aboriginal will be in 2157, analysing which county in the UK has the highest average milk consumption per household and counting how many times the Big Brother housemates sneeze.

And so this week I have started my class on the rocky road of data handling, though I hope to God that they don't have to use it too much in later life. I know how to work out the median, range or even standard deviation of a set of data and yet I'd feel pretty suicidal if I had a job that actually required me to use this knowledge. As far as I'm concerned it is one thing that some adults are forced to work in this field, it is quite another to start teaching it to eight year olds, especially as they probably won't use it in later life, especially as it is so uninspiring (and please don't say that it's the teacher's job to make it inspiring; even dressing up as a clown and singing the lesson would fail to raise statistics from the depths of tedium).

That, though, has not stopped me trying (trying to make it exciting, that is, not trying to sing in the lesson which, I can assure you, would not be entertaining for anyone). Starting with bar charts, I ignored the examples in the Numeracy Strategy (changes of temperature in London and Paris, numbers of birds visiting feeding stations . . . ) and made up a few of my own. From this I discovered that, as a class, their favourite cartoon is *Scooby Doo* with 12 votes, though *Yu-Gi-Oh* or however it's spelt, that bizarre Japanese creation whereby kids go round collecting cards of monsters, came worryingly high with eight votes. Finding out which football club they supported brought further disappointment. Manchester United came top with 18 votes, while Arsenal and Chelsea both featured highly. The local club, who provide coaching for the school, received exactly no votes – probably fair enough as they are pretty rubbish.

Once the class had drawn all this as neat charts in their books, we moved on to more statistical fun. Probability and percentages. Starting from the Strategy, the class made up sentences based on probability. In winter it will definitely be cold. In summer it could rain. Tomorrow there is an even chance that it will rain. For homework they made up some more probability sentences – my favourites being: 'When I get home my mum will definitely be eating doughnuts' and 'There is an even chance that mum will tell dad that he cannot go to the pub.' Using some of the data from the bar charts, the class then worked out some percentages. Forty-eight per cent of the class like *Scooby Doo*, 33 per cent have size one feet, 14 per cent chose sausage and chips as their favourite meal.

All of this would seem to be highly irrelevant to anything. Who cares what the average shoe size is, or what percentage of people like eating pizza and yet that is the lifeblood of data handling and the reason that it all seems so pointless. Just flicking through today's papers and supplements it is obvious that data handlers are always looming, analysing everything. Sixty-seven per cent of people recognize a picture of Sir Cliff Richard, 23 per cent of northerners put music on before making love, blue whales have the largest hearts of any mammal and, brilliantly, St John's Wood is the only Tube station whose name contains none of the letters of 'mackerel'. These facts and stats, though of passing curiosity, are probably only of genuine interest to those sad old men who record every single ball in cricket innings in leather-bound scorebooks. Going off on a tangent, I've always wondered what becomes of these scorecards, do they open them, years later, turn to a random page and go 'Kent v Sussex, 2002. Patel to Adams, dot ball. Ahh, I remember it well, turned slightly to off, Adams watched it go safely through to the "keeper". Ahh, another dot ball to follow, Adams mis-timed a cut straight to Fulton at Gully. Happy days . . . '

Among all this, for want of a better word, crap, the one piece of information that I could not find is what percentage of people want to make a living by handling data. All I have to go on is my own class and from that the result is nought per cent. Seven per cent want to be ballet dancers, three per cent rally drivers, six per cent chefs and 12 per cent either doctors or nurses. I find those results really encouraging – everyone wants to do something interesting. And perhaps data analysis can be useful afterall – it has helped reveal the ambitions and dreams of the class. I just hope that in a few years time another survey shows that a high percentage have achieved their goals.

# 43 Saying goodbye

Like a pub bouncer watching willowy Ali MacGraw pop her clogs in *Love Story*, I'm all of a quiver with mixed emotions today. In much the same way as a lifer eyes his release date, I had circled today's date months ago, expecting it to be greeted with a wave of elation, a huge party, regrettable acts of drunken abandon and a stonking hangover. Instead, I find that I face the same uncertainty as a person who, after 20 years inside, has stepped into a changed world full of baffling technological advances, ridiculous prices and previously unimaginable lifestyle choices. I half expect my future to consist of nothing more than double-bagging groceries into brown-paper bags at Joe's Grocery Store.

To clarify, and to get to the point after an introduction that was getting dangerously close to plagiarizing the *Shawshank Redemption*, today was my last in school – for now, at least. Back in September, it was a day that was hard to imagine ever actually happening. To get to it, I would first have to negotiate seven weeks in my first placement school and then an eight-week block in placement two, complete numerous essays and, most importantly, learn enough about teaching to prove that I wouldn't be a complete liability in the classroom.

The one thing of which I was fairly certain, and this is a feeling that only grew as the course progressed, was that I would be up for a party when it finally arrived. It would herald the end of planning, the end of early morning starts and the start of an extended summer holiday. And yet, now that the placement is over and I have a summer of leisure to look forward to, I feel strangely subdued. Walking out the school gates for the last time, I took one last long look back. I had only been in the school for eight weeks, too short a period I had thought to make much of a mark on me, but here I was feeling downcast at the prospect of not teaching the class again. Still, at least I left with plenty of little reminders of my time in school. The class had made and signed a giant card, and when they handed it over I felt a sudden mix of extreme gratitude and embarrassed regret – I had lambasted some of them only a couple of minutes earlier for being late to registration when, in hindsight, they were outside signing my leaving card.

As well as the giant card, I left with about a dozen cards made by individual pupils, a bottle of wine from the class teacher (though I got her a more expensive one in return) and numerous bits of coloured plastic, apparently called Scoobies, which are the new gift of choice from nine year olds. In this regard, I'm all for tradition, gifts should be in the form of chocolate, alcohol or, better still, money – getting more plastic doesn't feature highly on my list of priorities (though it does on Mrs Barbuti's).

On getting home, I also discovered that I had some unintentional souvenirs from school: a Year 5 literacy activity book, a guide to Jewish culture, an aerial photo of rural Cheshire and the school's pet rabbit. I should probably return these at some stage.

All in all, I thought I'd done pretty well for myself. The class seemed duly upset at my exit (though I'm sure they got over it in the space of minutes), the staff gave me warm goodbyes and I had gifts from the kids that, if not sellable on Ebay, at least showed that they cared.

More importantly, I have some great memories. Teaching lessons that had been met by more than just rows of blank faces, Friday afternoons spent on the school field taking rounders, a trip to the opera, and seeing the delight on their faces when they managed to build their own burglar alarms. It's these memories that I'll take from the placement to act as a far more lasting memento than any card, rabbit or bottle of wine.

In fact, the wine didn't last long at all – its lifespan from being unwrapped to poured down my gullet was somewhere shy of 30 minutes. That bottle will just be the first tonight. I said earlier in this column that I was feeling a bit subdued and disinclined to party. That feeling is being replaced by a warm glow, partly brought on by the alcohol and partly by the fact that this weekend, for the first time in months, will be completely free of planning. Instead it will be full of beer and sheep. Sorry, Freudian slip, I meant sleep. I might have loads of memories from school to take with me, but I have a feeling that memories of this weekend are going to be decidedly sketchy.

# 44 I've passed!

When I signed off from school last week just one thing stood between me and my fellow PGCE students and passing the course – a return trip to college to check that we had hit all of the standards. Judging by the number of texts that I received and sent this was a matter of some concern to all. Many of the standards were confidently crossed off months ago – e.g. teaching suitable literacy lessons – but others were harder to hit and the evidence of attaining them far sketchier. For planning an out-of-school learning experience all I had to show was helping out on a school visit to the opera, I had nothing to show for teaching art as a specialist came in to teach it, and for making effective use of teaching assistants I again had little to show because, although I had done it, I had forgotten to get it ticked off by the class teacher. Nevertheless, I put a tick in all the empty boxes, listed any evidence that seemed relevant (and evidence in these cases is pretty loose as it isn't necessarily corroborated by anything other than the student's memory), chucked in any loose sheet of paper I could find in order to bulk the file up and went in to college holding my breath.

Monday acted as a reprieve, no files were checked. Instead, after booking an appointment for folder checking for later in the week, we were treated to a Ploughman's lunch (though in my book a Ploughman's is never a treat – bread, cheese, pickle and apple for £4.95 in a pub always plays second fiddle to pie and chips) and a mini concert from a local school. The concert was pretty good, though there's something a bit disconcerting about primary school children singing 'They'll always be an England'. Monday evening was spent in the pub and, like all recent trips to the pub, the conversation centred on teaching. It's like that every time. On the walk to the pub we'll say something like 'right, I don't want to talk about bloody teaching' and then, as soon as we're sat down, we'll start talking about assessment, planning and inclusion. These conversations are definitely useful as you can learn so much from your peers, but it must make us look like the oldest bunch of 20-somethings in the world, Young Conservatives excepted.

On Tuesday, having booked an improbably early appointment with my tutor (and why do 8.30am appointments always look so appealing the day before – 'Ooh, it will leave the whole of the rest of the day free . . . ') I again turned up with files at the ready. About 90 minutes later, each appointment seemingly overrunning by about 200 per cent, I was finally in a suitable state of panic for the meeting which, as I saw it then, would decide my future. As with a trip to the doctor to sort out a persistent bowel problem, I walked in gingerly, not really knowing what to expect but imagining that it would involve a thorough, unwelcome but hopefully final probing.

The most likely scenario was that my tutor would call out every single standard, ask me what I had done to achieve it and then to show my evidence. Having rehearsed this scenario I imagined myself saying things such as 'well, I didn't quite' or 'you can ask my class teacher' or 'here's another tenner' a bit too regularly.

The reality was entirely different. Apparently in some universities, with some tutors, things happen as described above (though obviously without the bribes) and, while I can see the advantages of so thorough an approach I feel for the people forced to go through it. It's a bit like going through customs where most get to walk straight through, passport brazenly wafted under a few noses, while the unlucky few have their luggage scattered over an area the size of a football pitch and their bodies subjected to rubber-gloved scrutiny.

My tutor merely required evidence that I had a reasonable system in place and to ascertain this he asked only to see how I recorded evidence of hitting one standard. And I got to choose the standard. Naturally, I chose one that I had reams of evidence for (using ICT effectively, since you ask) and that was that, folder signed off. We then looked briefly at my Career Entry Profile – a folder you get towards the end of the course and in which you're meant to predict the future – where you'll be in 10 years, how many management points you'll have in 30 years, who'll win the 2049 FA Cup, that sort of thing.

All this had taken, at most, 5 minutes leaving me perplexed as to how all the other appointments had taken at least half an hour.

Should I have waffled on about future career options for longer, or perhaps asked where he thought I should take my career? No, I shouldn't, all I needed to do was sit back and enjoy a conversation about all things non-teaching – sport, the weather, trips to France and the workload of undergraduates.

And then, 20 minutes later, it was all over. I had expected a major grilling, but I also expected to come through the grilling with a sense of pride and, to use an Americanism, closure. Instead it was a major anti-climax. After eight weeks out of college we returned for a Ploughman's lunch and a brief chat.

And that really was that. An end-of-course social aside, teacher training was complete. Now that leaves just one small problem – finding a job in a county where there are no primary jobs on offer.

# 45 Job hunting

Congratulations on completing the course. Okay, you might not have officially finished yet, but I have absolutely no doubt that you're going to pass with flying colours. Now only one thing remains – finding your first job in teaching.

A few years ago this part would have been an absolute cakewalk. There were more teaching jobs than applicants absolutely everywhere so the graduating trainee could have their pick of them. Now things have turned, if not full circle, at least 90 degrees. In some places there are still authorities crying out for teachers, generally big, urban inner-city areas, especially in London, but in others there is a veritable drought of teaching jobs. However it is important not to worry. Accept that it might take a few interviews and lots of applications before you get a job and make sure you give yourself every chance.

One factor is your level of flexibility as to where you are willing to work. Obviously this might be dependent on other commitments, but if you are limited to working in a sparsely populated area your chances of finding permanent work are significantly reduced. For example, in Cheshire in the whole of April and May, a key time in job hunting, there were perhaps 40 primary jobs on offer. Take away from these the ones that were the wrong Key Stage, wanted a practising Catholic or were in completely the wrong part of Cheshire and there might have been a dozen suitable jobs for any trainee to apply for. In London, an area of roughly equivalent geographical size, the numbers would run into the hundreds, if not thousands.

To make it even harder in places like Cheshire, Cumbria, Kent and Norfolk, you will be competing in areas that are seen as something of a cushy job. If I had been teaching in Tower Hamlets or inner-city Birmingham for 30 years I would probably fancy a change and nowhere would seem nicer than the Broads, the Lakes, the Peak District or the Downs. And I would not be alone – for every job in these areas there are dozens of applicants, many from vastly experienced teachers who just fancy a move to a quieter location.

In contrast, if you are on a course in a, shall we say, less visually appealing area, the fact that there is a greater choice of jobs to apply for cannot fail but to work in your favour. If you don't have any ties to an area it is worth investigating which areas offer you the best chances of getting the job that you want. A simple flick through the *TES* will highlight the places that seem to have plenty of jobs going – these are places to focus your search.

As well as being flexible, it is important to start the search as early as possible. It is tempting to leave it until the course is all but over, but by then that dream job might well have already gone begging. The main reason to apply early is to make sure you get on the teaching pools. Many local authorities have a deadline for trainee teachers to apply for the pool – miss this and your chances of working in the area are vastly reduced. With the deadlines for pools ranging from early in the new year until April or May, it is worth taking time early on during the course to find out when the dates are and what the application process is. Finding this information will require nothing more than a visit to the local authority's website or a call to the education authority and once you have it you can develop a plan of action for getting that job. To get on a pool you will have to fill in an application form and attend an interview, but it's well worth it considering it could solve all your job-seeking worries. If selected, and a fair proportion of applicants end up on the pool, you may well end up with a number of job offers as schools go directly to the pool for their appointments rather than going through the whole rigmarole of advertising and then carrying out their own interviews. With pools, the more you can get on the better as, if you're fairly likely to get a job through being on one pool, you're almost bound to from getting on a selection of these.

It also doesn't pay to be too picky in looking for your first job. In an environment where a high proportion of trainees struggle to find employment, beggers really cannot afford to be choosers. If there is a job that looks vaguely suitable in your area go for it. At the very worst, it will hone your application writing skills and hopefully lead to an interview, while it could lead to a job offer. Realistically, your first job might not be perfect and while you should never take one which is gut-churningly nauseating you might have to take one that isn't Balamory. After a year's teaching you will be in a strong position to choose where you want to work, whether it is a better school in the same area, a worse school in the same area (there isn't a law banning sadists from becoming teachers), or even a language school in Italy – now there's an idea . . . To get to that stage you have to put in a year's hard graft as you learn your trade. To revert to a sporting analogy, you might have to be the YTS kid at Barnet before you get that dream move to Chelsea (though you won't be getting the equivalent Chelsea FC wage unless you opt to teach in Dubai (now there's another idea . . . ))

As with any job, preparation is crucial. Your application form needs to stand out. It is best to think of yourself as an American, boast as much as possible about every little achievement and proclaim yourself to be absolutely brilliant. After a few failed applications I discovered that it was my British reserve holding me back. My applications were well-written but I was losing out to people who admitted no errors and proclaimed themselves to be a super teacher. Everyone else going for the jobs you are going for will be selling themselves as shamelessly as an ad man shifting baby milk to Africa. You have to do the same.

Your application should also touch on key teaching issues such as differentiation and inclusion. Use examples to show off your knowledge in these areas, for instance in one application I described using a technique in literacy where in their tables of four, pupils would discuss answers and then nominate a spokesperson to answer – a form of Mind Friendly Learning that also boosted their speaking and listening and turn-taking skills. Having a theoretical knowledge of issues will only get you so far at this stage, it is important to be able to show that you have thought about issues in your teaching and classroom management.

It will focus your mind in writing the application if you think that you are trying to mention all the key issues, especially differentiation, behaviour management, inclusion, planning and assessment, and also to include examples of how you thought about these and melded the thought into your teaching.

Also, you don't want all the examples to come from any one subject – choose, e.g. a differentiation example from maths, an inclusion one from history and a planning one from science. This way your application becomes a nice blend of subjects and issues without resorting to the sort of sweeping generalized statements that are common in ill-thought-out applications.

With a perfect application, interviews will inevitably follow, and again preparation is the key. Teaching interviews are similar in content to the pre-course interviews in that there are no trick questions or requests to answer in the style of a French DJ. The interviewers – plural because as well as the head there are likely to be at least two other interested parties presently drawn from other school staff, the Governors and, conceivably the Local Education Authority, or, in the case of a CofE school, the church – want to get to know your character. Unlike in most jobs, you are not being paid just to fulfil a task, you are being paid because your character is suitable for the responsibility of looking after 30 youngsters. The interviewers are testing your competence to teach as well as your general, for want of a better word, niceness. They want someone keen, eager to learn and, most importantly, someone who can expand to fulfil a larger role the longer they stay at the school. Questions, therefore tend to be fairly open ended, such as: 'Tell me about a lesson you taught that went well', 'Tell me about a lesson that went badly' (try and limit the answer to this to one lesson), 'How would you cope with a child who continually disrupted the lesson?', 'What do you take differentiation to mean?'

The questions almost have an essay-like feel, but don't be fooled into giving answers packed full of answers quoting textbooks. At this stage you need to be able to give practical examples, similar to the ones you used in your application. In fact, in writing the application it is worth thinking of two examples for each issue – one for the letter and one for the interview as the interview should be more than just a recital of what they may, or may not, have already read.

The other big question they will have is you – what are you like and what have you to offer other than teaching? This is your chance to talk about all those clubs you are a member of (and if you're not in one, join quickly), those trips around the world and your interesting hobbies. Charity work is especially valuable, showing that you are someone keen to give of yourself. A few weekends spent selling clothes in Oxfam would be time well-spent if it proved to be the little extra that lands you a great job.

Talking of good investments, you should be buying the *TES* every week towards the end of the course, or at least going to the website regularly. It is the best single source of jobs and easily searchable. However, there are plenty of other resources out there to help. One of the most useful is the college noticeboard. Jobs will get posted here that may not even be advertised anywhere else, boosting your chances greatly. Tutors may also tell the course about jobs in the middle of lectures or tutorials at the end of the course so it is important to turn up, even if only on the off-chance that a job in your area might be mentioned.

The final resource that really can't be missed is the local authority's website. Usually updated daily, this is the first place that new jobs in your area will be posted, complete with full application details and deadline dates. In some areas you can even apply online, though a personal call first is always wise if only to put you in the head's mind as an application worth looking out for.

Using these resources, your great application letter and a charming interview technique, hopefully you will land a job without too many tribulations. If you don't you have some tough questions to ask yourself. The main one, with the number of jobs thinning out, is how you are going to find employment. One option is to widen the search and think about any areas you have previously been steering clear of, or even areas that would require a complete relocation.

Another option is to consider supply teaching. In urban areas, going on the supply pool is likely to lead to virtual full-time employment and potentially, a few months in, a choice of job offers to choose between. However, in more rural areas where there are no staff jobs going it is unrealistic to expect supply teaching to be much more fruitful. In these areas the odds on employment of any kind are reduced due to the sheer numbers of applicants relative to every job.

A third option, one taken by a friend, is to bite the bullet and move abroad, in his case taking a TEFL post in Barcelona. Undeniably, this would be a brilliant job, just don't make the switch for the wrong reasons. Barcelona, Milan or Dubai would be a lonely place if it was a move rushed into with no real thought. To make a real go of it, it would have to be an option you had ALWAYS thought of taking.

And the final option is to seek employment in another profession. On the course we were advised to not do this under any circumstances, but such a patronizing viewpoint is easier to make when you don't have the pressure of needing any form of job simply to pay the bills. Seeking alternative employment can be either a short-term option, keeping you ticking over until another assault on teaching in January or September. Equally, you might decide to apply for other jobs and decide to stick with whatever profession comes your way.

Either way it really doesn't matter as long as you are happy with the outcome and your decision. The course is a once in a lifetime experience regardless of the outcome. It is to be enjoyed and cherished, as is whatever comes next. I wish you every success.